EDI – The rout
lean production

GW01035981

The management guide

By John Hartley
Edited by John Mortimer

Industrial Newsletters Ltd, Dunstable, Beds LU5 6BS, UK

First published in Great Britain in 1991 by
Industrial Newsletters Ltd, 42 Market Square, Toddington, Dunstable, Beds LU5 6BS, UK

Copyright © 1991 by John Hartley and John Mortimer

All rights reserved. No part of this publication may be reproduced, stored in a retrieval system, or transmitted, in any form or by any means, electronic, mechanical, photocopying, recording or otherwise, without the prior permission of the copyright owners.

British Library Cataloguing in Publication Data
available on request

Cover design: Mark Mortimer

ISBN 1 873381 02 6

Manufactured in the United Kingdom

Printed by Jetspeed Printing Services Ltd., 3 Roundwood Lane, Harpenden, Herts. AL5 3BW

Foreword

CURRENT applications of EDI in manufacture are fairly narrow, and their primary function is to support the supply of components. Its true potential is much wider, but a full understanding of the marketplace is necessary to gain real advantage from the technique.

Manufacturers are increasingly facing global competition, and need to operate in a worldwide marketplace. To do so successfully, companies need to change significantly the way they relate to markets, the way they organise design and manufacture, and the way they co-operate with customers, suppliers and consortia partners.

Trading through the supply chain is evolving into a series of partnerships in which information exchange is the medium for integration of design, manufacture, distribution and customer service processes. These information flows are best effected by EDI. To succeed and survive, manufacturing companies have to exploit the potential of EDI to the full.

Lucas has installed EDI widely to support its trading operations around the world and will continue to exploit its potential wherever it is of commercial value.

Keith Blacker

Past Chairman, EDI Association
Lucas Engineering & Systems Ltd
Shirley
Solihull.

EDI—the enabling technology

EDI (electronic data interchange) is a unique business tool that enables manufacturing companies to change the way they operate. It automates communications between manufacturers and their vendors and distributors, and therefore allows companies to strengthen and streamline the supply chain into an efficient, flexible force capable of matching the world's best. Moreover, the use of EDI enables managers to rethink their businesses—it is the gateway to new opportunities.

Manufacturers that adopt EDI are able to cut the fat from administration and materials handling while increasing the efficiency of those functions. With the combination of EDI and just-in-time to reshape deliveries from vendors, and *kanban* systems in their plants, lean production, in which waste is cut from all aspects of manufacture—from downtime between batches of products to scrap materials—becomes a reality. Thus, although EDI is an important tool in its own right, it is also a key enabling technology leading the way to world-class manufacture.

Contents

Chapter One

EDI—a better way of doing business

A strategic technology for restructuring

Essential control for Just-in-Time deliveries

Increases sales, cuts costs of supply process

EDI (Electronic Data Interchange) is the enabling technology no business can afford to ignore. It opens up new opportunities, and at the same time sharpens competition for existing participants in any market. Initially, EDI helps reduce the costs of administration, allowing the office to be automated in the same way that robotics automated the factory. Machines can talk to machines, performing many tasks without error at high speed, 24 hours a day, 365 days a year.

More significantly, EDI paves the way to 'lean production' or 'lean manufacture', as no other technique can. Although it operates between the manufacturer and its vendors and distributors, its use influences many aspects of manufacture, enabling changes necessary to achieve world-class manufacture to be made.

EDI is a technique that allows managers with foresight and imagination to make dramatic improvements to the performance of their company, and should not be considered as one more aspect of IT (information technology) best left to the technicians. On the contrary, it is a way of doing business that mainstream managers need to control.

EDI not only streamlines administration, but also:

☐ Reduces non-productive costs by cutting the number
   of personnel and the space needed for administration
   drastically;
☐ Is essential for Just-in-Time (JIT) deliveries;
☐ Helps reduce stock levels, in some cases by 50-75%;
☐ Shows up and helps eliminate waste;
☐ Brings flexibility to manufacture throughout the
   supply chain.

These are all prerequisites to lean production. EDI is the
catalyst that gives manufacturers the opportunity of
restructuring their businesses to reach world class levels
of quality, productivity and lead time.

Typical of the way in which EDI changes business
methods is with routine orders and invoices. The
processes are not just automated: many are obliterated.
They are replaced by self-billing invoices and orders
triggered automatically. Therefore, fewer operations are
required to carry out a business transaction. EDI plays a

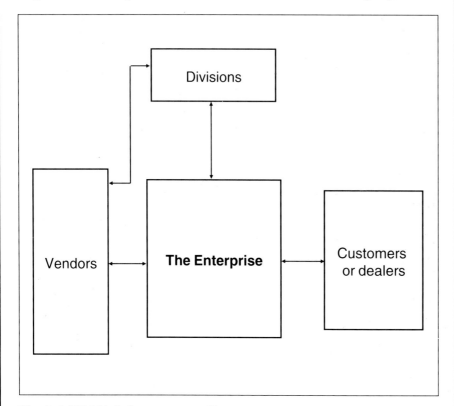

Fig.1.1 EDI link between trading partners

broader role than that of automation itself; it enables managers to simplify operations and rethink the way in which they do business.

EDI helps companies meet change

Imaginative managers will find EDI opens up new opportunities. They can reshape their business, improving links with their suppliers. They can serve customers they were previously unable to reach, or change from centralised management to a distributed approach or vice versa, depending on how their business world is changing.

Although some of the pioneers of EDI used it to reshape retail businesses—indeed it is the enabling technology most responsible for changing the face of retailing in Britain—manufacturers have most to gain from the technique.

EDI is an important ingredient in the move from multiple sourcing and the adversarial relationship engendered by that situation to single sourcing. With single sourcing and the close co-operation brought about by EDI, overall performance of the supply chain can be improved, to the benefit of both vendor and customer. This move is one of the sea of changes essential for manufacturing industry in the UK to match and maintain world-class levels of innovation, quality, cost, and response to the customer.

With EDI, managers have far more information at their fingertips about deliveries, and future requirements, when changes in specification are required, and a host of other factors than they would have with paper trading. They will find therefore the implementation of improved manufacturing strategies based on flexible automation is more effective than hitherto. Nor will they find the babel of different languages—not to mention complete absence of any language—they found when they tried to interconnect robots, logic controllers and NC machines in the early days. There are different languages, but these can be translated readily and automatically.

Vital element in JIT

One of the most important uses of EDI in manufacture is to expedite JIT (Just-in-Time)—indeed, most users of JIT consider EDI an indispensible feature of a JIT programme. Because up-to-date information is exchanged and deliveries are more reliable with EDI, the level of confidence between vendor and customer is increased. In the USA, the Big Three car makers, General Motors (GM), Ford and Chrysler, used EDI with JIT to cut the value of the stock held in their plants by $1 billion in the period 1980 to 1989, and have a target of using EDI to cut the cost of production of a car by $300. Dramatic gains have also been made in the UK by the Rover Group.

EDI is also helping multi-national companies supply any market from any plant according to the patterns of demand and cost. Plants for small products no longer need to be sited near a market; with investigation of costs and control of deliveries electronically, it is practical to use the most appropriate plant for each product or market.

Process and chemical industries are starting to use EDI to streamline their operations, while EDI will help manufacturers gain more reliable service, with accurate tracing, from freight forwarders and haulage companies. Thus, the benefits of EDI extend to a wide range of business activities.

Many companies have made significant gains in operating efficiency thanks to EDI. For example, administration, often seen as a necessary evil, can now be pared down in the same way that manning levels have been reduced in the factory.

In the USA, where EDI first took root, one company exploited EDI to increase market share by 17% a year for several years while doubling the productivity/employee. Another US manufacturer found that EDI increased sales by 30% because its use increased the availability of products. Yet another company was able to cut the time involved in the preparation of purchase orders by 93%.

Transmission from computer to computer

So what is EDI? It involves the transmission of data between one company and another and is defined as:

☐ *The exchange of structured data from one computer application to another by telecommunications.*

Although EDI can be used effectively between branches or divisions of one company, the main benefit ensues when it is used between different companies through a telecommunications network, since this use enables the way of doing business to be changed.

Structured data are those drawn from an application in a computer, converted to a standard format and then transmitted. Subsequently, the data format is translated back to that of the application.

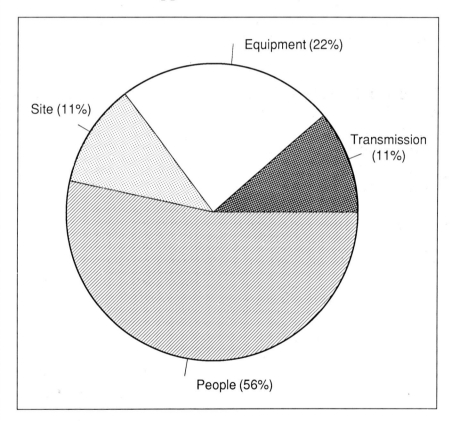

Equipment (22%)

Site (11%)

Transmission (11%)

People (56%)

Fig.1.2 People account for the bulk of the cost of paper trading

The standard format is essential, since the ultimate aim with EDI is for any company to be able to trade electronically with any other—in the same way that anyone can telephone or send a fax to any company anywhere. In the short term, a company may trade electronically with only a few partners but after a year or two it may need to trade electronically with others in different industries in different countries. For this reason, custom-made message formats and protocols would be hopeless; once a company needed to trade with one in another industry, it would require a different file format, and possibly a different computer. So, the use of standard formats is mandatory.

It is important to recognise that EDI is a transmission between computers. It should not be confused with electronic mail (E-mail), for example. E-mail is an important medium, but it is a way of communications between people. It may be used to supplement EDI, in the same way that the telephone is used to supplement paperwork; but it is not EDI.

Nor is transfer of structured data from computer to computer with subsequent printing out and manual rekeying into an application true EDI. This is not an academic distinction, because the benefits of EDI come only when people think in terms of automating operations, not merely transferring data more quickly than the postman.

High manual cost of paperwork

EDI is much more than just automated mail. It is an enabling technology that helps entrepreneurs and managers grasp new opportunities in a decade of challenge and change.

But the automation of many administrative chores comes first—and one reason they are performed relatively inefficiently is that they are repetitive. How often does the managing director, hurrying to a meeting, glance into the accounts department, and wonder why it looks so chaotic, and why so many people are needed just to execute orders and process invoices?

It looks chaotic because most of the time and effort involved are spent in correcting errors in invoices, reconciling them with orders, and obtaining duplicates of papers that have been lost in the post, rendered illegible by spilled coffee or by a poor facsimile transmission. When paperwork is handled manually, it is these errors and losses that push up the cost.

A survey carried out in 1984 by AT&T Istel and the Institute of Physical Distribution Management found that there were some 3.2 billion documents involved in the order/invoice cycle in the UK annually, and that the average processing cost of each document was £10, to give a gross cost of £32 billion. By 1990, the growth in the economy and in inflation would have taken the costs up to over £50 billion. Significantly, over 50% of these costs are labour. In the US, the cost of processing a purchase order manually is put at $30-50.

Generally, EDI is used first to automate the delivery of invoices or orders, with advice notes and delivery information coming next. It is not surprising that with the high costs of manual processing users of EDI report big savings. For example, one large North American company found that it was sending 1.3 million purchase orders to its seven major vendors each year. With the adoption of EDI to transmit the orders to just these seven companies, it saved $45 million a year. Hewlett Packard's German subsidiary found that EDI reduced the time purchasing officers spent on administration by 25-40% so the cost of purchase orders and confirmation was slashed by 66%. Navistar was able to save $5/business communication. Daimler-Benz, which adopted EDI for the top 200 of its 1,800 vendors, was able to cut its manual labour costs by over 15%.

Purchase order costs cut by 75%

Other examples of the savings include Digital Equipment with a 75% reduction in the cost of the preparation of purchase orders, while Pratt and Whitney, the aerospace company, cut the cost of a purchase order by $30. With 310 of its suppliers using EDI, it has eliminated the need for 300,000 paper documents a year, while its orders are accepted in three days instead of the seven or eight days

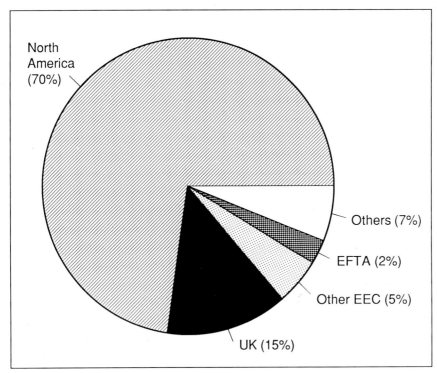

Fig.1.3. The biggest number of users of EDI are in North America, the UK, and Australasia, which accounts for most users shown as 'Others'. 'Other EC' is the EC excluding the UK

encountered with paper orders. GTE cut the time involved in the preparation of purchase orders by no less than 93%.

Meanwhile, the US oil industry has taken up EDI for many inter-company transactions, and expects that the annual savings will amount to a staggering $500 million annually.

In the UK, the Rover Group found that EDI cut the number of invoices rejected because of errors from 30%—a typical industry level—to 3%. Meanwhile, British Coal has been able to identify cost-savings of £50,000 a year, mainly through reduced costs in handling invoices, and chasing urgent orders. It too found a dramatic reduction in incorrect invoices from 30% to 5%.

There are many other examples of the cost savings that come from EDI, but to gain those savings the processes must be automated—manual intervention must be limited to where it is essential. The need for the minimum human intervention in EDI cannot be over-emphasised; it is one reason why many companies are unable to prove that EDI will save money before they start operating. Because the method of operation changes with EDI, some costs cannot be quantified until EDI is being used.

To companies led by people with vision, who are ready to change their operations to seize opportunities, cost cutting is but the fringe benefit of EDI. The real benefits come when they analyse what EDI will allow them to do.

Among the exciting gains achieved by EDI are those of American Hospital Systems and Benetton. American Hospital Systems supplies consumables and medical equipment to hospitals, and decided to transfer the cost of order entry to its customers by providing them with terminals. Initially, the aim was to reduce overheads, but since the system enabled hospital staff to interrogate stock records and prices, and thus gain quicker service, they soon found it much easier to obtain supplies from American Hospital Systems than from other vendors.

As a result, American Hospital Systems increased market share at the rate of 17% a year, while productivity/ employee increased from $61,000 to $115,000.

Benetton's approach was to install Electronic Point Of Sale (EPOS) terminals at all its outlets, well ahead of the herd, and to hold undyed cloth and garments so that as it received data on actual sales it could decide what colours were required, make up batches to dye and supply them to the retailer without the need for orders. It was able to keep the shops stocked with the products people wanted, moving automatically as fashion changed, and so grew at the rate of 50% a year for 10 years.

Business up eightfold, stock down 50%

Tesco is another company that has used EDI to change the type of stores it operates, and the way it does business with its suppliers. In doing so it has upgraded its role from that of a supplier of cheap goods in stores decorated to a low level to a supplier of quality goods sold in pleasant superstores. As a result it has increased market share significantly.

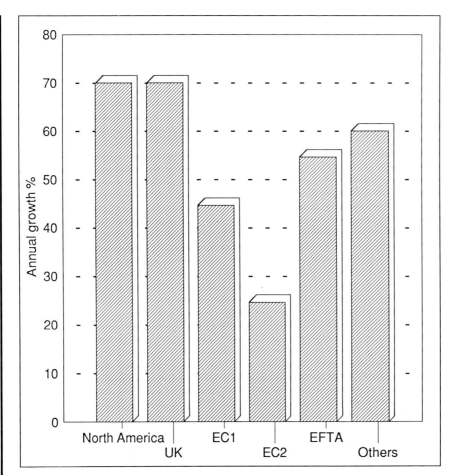

Fig.1.4 The use of EDI is growing fastest in North America and the UK, and more slowly elsewhere in the EC. 'EC1' consists of Denmark, Germany and The Netherlands; 'EC2' the remaining members of the EC, excluding the UK

For example, thanks largely to the use of EDI it has been able to increase the number of items of food sold from 5,000 in 1982 to 16,000 in 1990, while adding wines and many other items to its lists. In this time, the volume of business has increased from 50 million cases to 400 million cases a year. Nevertheless, the stock levels have been decreased by 50% but the level of availability has increased from 92% to 98%. Clearly, such a rate of expansion would have been extremely difficult to achieve without the efficiency of EDI.

Most of the success stories involve large companies, while many smaller ones adopted EDI because their largest customer asked or insisted that they did so. Already, 500 of *The Times* Top 1000 Companies in the UK are using EDI, and managers in smaller companies might well wonder whether EDI is just for big corporations. Is it really worthwhile for small companies as well?

At first, it was the large companies that inevitably made the waves by taking the initiative and deciding to adopt EDI. Companies such as Marks & Spencer, Tesco, B&Q, Ford, ICI, Rover Group, British Coal and Black and Decker decided to use EDI, and persuaded their largest suppliers to do likewise. In this way, a number of EDI communities have developed, with the major manufacturer or retailer as the hub to which an increasing number of companies are connected by spokes. Therefore, many small companies are involved, and they can benefit equally as well as large companies. Moreover, there is plenty of experience from which new users may draw.

The number of users of EDI are reaching critical mass, while new users are joining existing EDI communities at quite a rate, so it is much easier to start than a few years ago. Now, few of the communities are self-contained, with some vendors to B&Q for example also supplying Rover Group or British Coal.

Surveys suggest that the use of EDI is now growing rapidly in the USA and Europe where the UK is continuing its lead. According to Frost & Sullivan, the market in the USA will grow from $141 million in 1990 to $750 million in 1995. Significantly, the survey showed that the market for PC software will grow fastest, as the role of PCs increases at the expense of larger computers.

Value of EDI services, USA, 1990 and 1995, ($m)		
	1990	1995
Total	141	752
Network services	92	413
Professional services	19	75
Software:		
Mainframes	12	75
Minicomputers	11	54
PCs	19	135

An EEC study forecast that within the next 20 years the volume of EDI in the EC will reach 50 billion documents a year, while Pan-European Forecasts puts the value of the business at $1.5 billion by 1993. The spur for

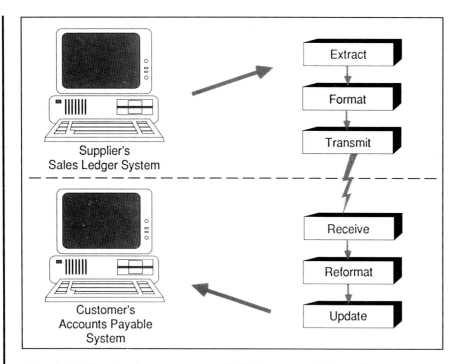

*Fig. 1.5. The basic processes of EDI are carried out by
computers*

this growth will come from interlinking between
different communities, with vendors being able to trade
electronically with several major customers.

Ovum, a British consultancy, foresees substantial growth
in Europe, with the total market increasing from $86
million in 1990 to $396 million in 1994, indicating
a significant movement.

Expected growth in EDI services in Europe, ($m)

	1990	1992	1994
Services	35	96	213
Package software	18	38	70
Custom software	10	21	42
Consultancy and training	23	46	71
Total	86	201	396

The UK will maintain its lead in EDI usage, according to
Ovum, with its market increasing from $47 million in
1990 to $169 million in 1994—more than the combined
market forecast for France and Germany.

EDI started in the USA, where there are currently some 10,000 users, against 3,500 in the UK, around 1,500 in the rest of Europe, and over 2,000 in Australia. The number of users is growing rapidly, at about 70% a year in the UK, and at over 50% in the USA, Canada, EFTA countries and Australasia. In Europe, the UK is the current leader in the availability of networks, in the number of users, and in reaping the benefits of EDI.

However, only a very small proportion of companies are using EDI now, so there is considerable opportunity to move in and use this tool strategically. Continental companies are taking a strategic approach to EDI whereas the approach is predominantly re-active in the UK. Therefore, British manufacturing industry needs to change it attitude if it is to maintain the lead and use EDI as a true enabling technology.

Requirements for EDI

So what is needed to implement EDI? The first requirement is management commitment; to use it strategically rather than to cut costs. The aim must be:

☐ To improve the supply chain in its entirety;
☐ To improve relationships with customers and suppliers;
☐ To help find new markets, or ways of increasing competitiveness.

The involvement of top management really is essential if the benefits are to be gained.

In hardware, the minimum investment is for a PC and modem and some software at a cost from £1,500 upward, but of course this must be backed up with the correct training for the personnel involved.

There are many ways in which EDI messages can be transmitted: they can be sent over a dedicated leased line to a partner, over the telephone line or through a value added network (VAN). Nearly all EDI messages in the UK are sent through a VAN. The principal VAN services for EDI in the UK are AT&T Istel's AT&T EDI, (formerly Edict), INS Tradanet and IBM Information Network. These networks provide store-and-forward services, with a number of ancillaries, such as translation between different standards.

To send a message by EDI, the sender carries out a series of operations at a computer. He or she:

☐ Accesses a file from an application in the computer system;
☐ Converts it to the desired message format;
☐ Sends it over a telephone line or a leased line to the network.

The network receives the messages and places it in the appropriate 'mailbox'—actually a file in a directory in a computer—to await collection by the recipient. Later, the recipient interrogates the mailbox for new messages, and downloads the file, translates it to the application file format, and carries out the necessary action.

The advantage of this system is that one company can sort out its requirements during the day and send the order to a vendor in the evening or overnight for action the following morning.

Although the technology of EDI is well-proven, EDI is in its infancy compared with telephony. Nevertheless, there are technical problems to be solved. New users need to decide what hardware and software and which VAN to use, as well as which of the standards for protocols and syntax. It is necessary to address these matters with a sound technical approach, and managers must expect the introduction of EDI to take time. However, these are merely the problems that provide engineers with a raison d'etre, and should not be used to obscure the potential benefits of EDI.

The potential benefits are limited not by the technology—which is in any case developing rapidly—but by the imagination and ambition of senior management and their staff. Managers ready to implement changes and to follow through those changes as the benefits multiply will gain most. Those that expect to cut costs to the bone without tackling other problems in their business will find that although the benefits are worthwhile, they are overtaken by more imaginative competitors.

Chapter Two

Manufacturers profit from EDI

EDI reduces administrative costs

Cuts lead time by 8-10 days immediately

Pro-active use ensures maximum benefits

WHAT sort of manufacturer will gain from EDI, and in what circumstances should a company adopt EDI? There are no limits to the type of business that can benefit from EDI, so long as a fair number of invoices and orders are handled, and there are a number of principal customers or suppliers. But it is broader than that; some very small companies that have set themselves the target of exploiting EDI have grown substantially as a result of investing in it.

However, many companies will soon find that the use of EDI is virtually essential for some aspects of their business. For example, on 1 January 1993, electronic records will be accepted throughout the EC instead of paper, and at the same time, H.M. Customs & Excise is due to insist that all companies exporting from the UK to other countries in the EC submit the documentation by EDI. H.M.Customs & Excise will also expect to receive all data for statistical records on exports and imports to be furnished by EDI. It is no wonder therefore that Hugh Norton, managing director, British Petroleum Co plc said that 'no company involved in pan-European operations could afford to ignore EDI.'

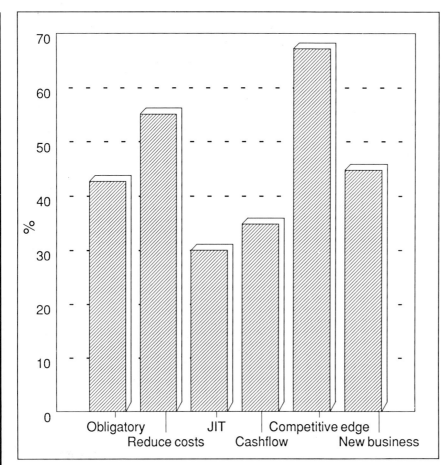

Fig.2.1. Most users of EDI put increased competitive edge as the main reason for its use

Compulsory EDI

Apart from meeting the requirements of H.M. Customs & Excise, some manufacturers will find EDI becoming compulsory elsewhere. First, there is the CALS (Computer Aided Acquisition and Logistics Support) programme launched by the US Department of Defence (DoD) which requires that all data for new weapons systems be transmitted by EDI from 1992—initially by magnetic tape. The ultimate aim is for the data to be be held in distributed databases, and military personnel calling up the relevant sections of a manual by EDI.

This move affects all companies in the USA involved in military equipment, and their suppliers in a variety of industries. In addition, some European companies supply North American military suppliers, and therefore will be obliged to use EDI. For example, British Aerospace (BAe) supplies the US DoD, and has decided to adopt the CALS methodology; it expects its larger European suppliers to do so as well. In addition, the French armaments industry signed an agreement with the US DoD in April 1991 to develop EDI for use in its transactions.

There are three stages extending to 1997 in the CALS plan and, with the aid of EDI and simultaneous engineering, the DoD expects to save $39 billion in the period 1992-6.

In addition to the Customs and Excise and DoD, many large European manufacturers and retail groups are insisting—with varying degrees of force—that their vendors use EDI. However, so long as senior management takes the right approach, this compulsion is not a disadvantage since the benefits of EDI to manufacturing industry far outweigh the cost and complication. EDI helps a company improve its effectiveness in several ways, and all are extremely important at any time, but could well prove to be a lifeboat in a stormy recession.

First, EDI improves operating efficiency by:

- ☐ Cutting administrative costs;
- ☐ Reducing the lead time required to handle orders;
- ☐ Tracing the progress of deliveries once they are in the hands of a carrier;
- ☐ Improving the response to customers' orders or enquiries;
- ☐ Enabling the method of purchasing and receiving goods, or of receiving orders and despatching goods to be restructured.

It also enables companies to rethink the way they operate, and to make fundamental changes. This is the exciting aspect of EDI, and it will follow a determined effort to implement EDI to improve efficiency. EDI gives the opportunity to:

- ☐ Improve links with vendors, and increase trust;
- ☐ Reduce stock levels, speed-up deliveries from vendors, and implement JIT;
- ☐ Seek out new methods of doing business and new markets.

Reactive mode the worst

Many companies adopt EDI to comply with a directive
from a dominant customer, such as a major retail chain
or a vehicle manufacturer. This is certainly the worst
situation in which to adopt EDI. Inevitably, the vendor
considers the necessity of invoicing or accepting orders
by EDI an on-cost required to maintain an important
contract. The company will be unlikely to explore other
benefits, since its attitude is likely to remain negative,
unless management has vision. More likely, management
will be glad to have retained the contract, and leave it at
that.

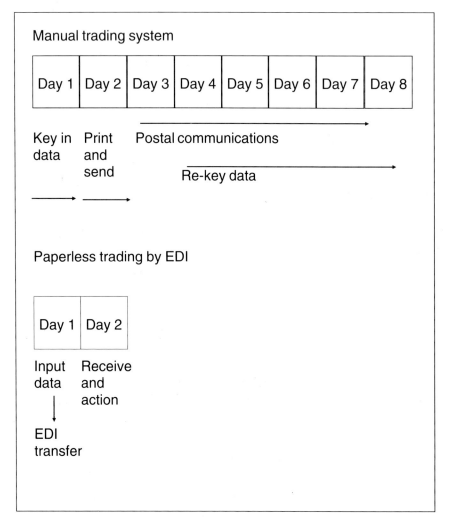

*Fig.2.2. EDI guarantees quick delivery of documents, saving
several days compared with the post*

More dangerous is the situation when a large company tells its smaller vendors that although it would like them to use EDI it is not obligatory. The small vendors heave sighs of relief and forget all about EDI— and to their cost. After the customer has invested heavily in EDI, and has a smooth system operating, it will find that it is left with a relatively large staff to handle a tiny proportion of its business, perhaps with 100 to 500 vendors.

As soon as there is pressure on margins, the management will investigate where overheads can be cut. Paperwork will come into sharp focus, simply because it accounts for the bulk of work the department handles, but for a small amount of business. Either the customer will then insist on the use of EDI for all vendors, or it will 'recommend' that orders to small companies be channeled through a factor that is big enough to use EDI. Either way, the small vendor is likely to lose out. If it installs an EDI system, it is doing so under pressure, not at a time when its customer is anxious to help vendors cope with the inevitable teething troubles.

Therefore, all vendors that supply major manufacturers or retailers should adopt EDI so that they are ready to trade electronically before they are asked to do so, and can gain from its use in other areas. In doing so, they should seek out ways in which EDI can improve their business—from the simplification of the forms they use for invoices and orders, to making contact with new customers and suppliers.

Even small companies that receive orders monthly or even quarterly can find EDI worthwhile. Some of British Coal's EDI users are very small, with one having only eight employees. One small EDI user is Mark Sawmills, Somerset, which has two mills supplying British Coal with chocks, the wooden blocks used to support the roof in the tunnels underground. The company is enthusiastic about EDI, despite the fact that routine orders come through only four times a year. Paperwork is reduced, there are no delays in the mail, and fewer errors. The company purchased an inexpensive software package from Compower, a British Coal subsidiary, and found it efficient and easy to use.

Manufacturing industries switch to EDI

Any substantial business, and many small ones, should start planning to use EDI if they are not already doing so. New users will almost certainly find some trading partners are ready to join them.

Although individual companies led the use of EDI in the retail industry, in several cases industries set up committees to produce standards so that the use of EDI could be implemented generally. For example, the British Society of Motor Manufacturers and Traders (SMMT) and its European counterparts established the Odette (Organisation for Data Exchange by Tele-Transmission in Europe) project in the motor industry in 1984. It has since been adopted by 350 companies in the UK and 550 elsewhere in Europe.

Following a separate move by ICI, leading European chemical companies established a set of messages for EDI, while European electronics companies also moved together toward EDI; in addition, the UK construction industry set up the Edicon group. Now, EDI is in use in a large number of industries in the UK, Europe and the USA, including:

- ☐ Air freight operators;
- ☐ Builders' merchants and the construction industry;
- ☐ Electronics industry;
- ☐ Engineering companies;
- ☐ Motor vehicle manufacturing industry;
- ☐ Office equipment suppliers;
- ☐ Publishers and distributors of magazines;
- ☐ Road transport hauliers;
- ☐ Shipping and freight forwarding;
- ☐ Suppliers of chemicals.

Some of these have many well-established communities, whereas some of the others are still conducting trials. But whatever the state of play, all industries are confident that EDI represents the only way forward.

Financial settlements can be made by EDI, but this is at an early stage as yet, not least because many companies are not keen to pay their bills sooner than they do at present. However, Barclays and Lloyds already offer an

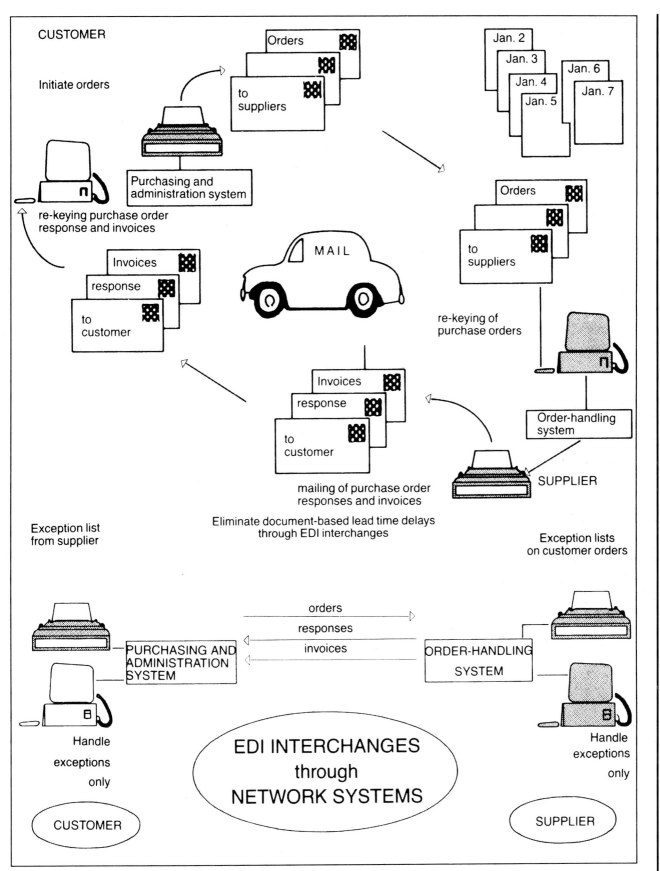

Fig. 2.3. Far fewer operations are involved with EDI than with paperwork

EDI payments service, and by 1992, the five main British banks will be offering customers an integrated system for the payment of cheques, reducing the cost of a cheque from £5-20 to about £3. This will close the business loop, and make EDI almost inescapable for any manufacturer.

Basic benefits

The basic advantages of EDI result from the speed and simplicity with which orders and invoices can be sent. At worst, an order will be received one day after it is sent. This contrasts with the conventional system, which requires:

- ☐ Two days to process the order in-house;
- ☐ Two to four days in the post;
- ☐ One or two days waiting to be re-entered into the computer of the vendor.

Therefore, it is not surprising that Hewlett Packard, with the aid of EDI, was able to cut the processing costs of its accounts payable department in New York by 38%, and that the US Department of Transportation cut the cost of a purchase order from $50 to $7. Westinghouse claimed that EDI led to a 90% reduction in the time spent tracing shipments, while Super Valu Stores of the US quotes visible savings of $300,000 a year. So there is no doubt that costs can be cut drastically.

In a survey of British users carried out by the National Computing Centre, over 50% of respondents considered cost saving an important reason for using EDI. However, 68% were looking for an increased competitive edge, and 45% expected to be able to win new business. Indeed, the big winners with EDI almost all agree that the cost-savings are significant but incidental—the real benefits come from the new ways in which they can operate their businesses.

Priorities with EDI

The first priority, given the decision to implement EDI, is for senior management to take the lead—whether the company has 10,000 or 10 employees—and to ferret out ways of using it to improve relations with its vendors and customers, increase added value and market coverage, find new niche markets it could not previously reach, jump ahead of its competitors, and to streamline operations generally.

The second priority is to find a person who can push this important approach to business through; he or she should not be an IT technologist, but rather a manager with some understanding of the technology. Then it is preferable to set up a multi-functional team to make sure that the real benefits spread right through the organisation. It is then up to the technical staff to turn those ideas into reality, and only with this sort of preparation can they provide the best solutions. With this positive approach, management can look forward to the streamlined operations that come with lean manufacture, and the new opportunities that follow.

Chapter Three

How EDI changed the face of retailing

Tesco restructures with EDI

More variety, lower stock, greater availability

Big manufacturer regains trade with small shops

SEVERAL big retailers have used EDI to alter the structure of their business with considerable success, and this sector differs from others in that these companies worked alone to set up their own EDI communities. Of course, they needed to find a network and common standards for messages, but there has not been the industry-wide co-operation evident elsewhere. Instead, the co-operation has been between the retailer and its major suppliers.

Although some suppliers feel the co-operation was rather one-sided, there are cases where close co-operation has changed the relationship between supplier and retailer substantially—and for the better.

Generally, the messages used between retailers and suppliers are confined to invoices, orders and delivery instructions, with some of the leaders now using Just-in-Time (JIT) concepts for deliveries to their superstores.

Some managers in manufacturing companies may doubt the value of the experience of retailers, but in practice, the logistics of the operators and superstores are similar to those of manufacturers, and logistics is a key area offering scope for slimming operations down. Both rely on a large number of vendors to supply them with a wide variety of goods, and the customers of both are demanding greater variety all the time.

Like the manufacturer, the retailer requires some products—perishables—to be delivered at short notice to JIT schedules. Other items are delivered less frequently, but shortages result in lost business— just as they result in a financial loss in manufacture. The retailer takes the products through a number of stages until they arrive on the shelves in the superstores. From then on, the retailer loses control—unlike the manufacturer—and has to trust that his forecast of demand was accurate.

Then, the customer of a modern superstore behaves in the way that the manufacturer will in the EDI age. He calls off the products he wants by picking them from the shelves, and self-bills by allowing the goods to be passed through the check-out. Finally, he may then pay by Switch so that his account is debited, and the superstore credited immediately. Clearly, the logistics and changes being made in the retail industry have many parallels in manufacture.

Seize opportunities

Now, many different sectors of the retail business are using EDI, such as brewers, builders merchants, car accessory shops, food shops, newsagents, and record shops. The impetus has come from large companies, many of which are operating with a small number of partners.

As mentioned in Chapter One, American Hospital Systems (AHS) and Benetton are two outstanding examples of success in this sector. In both cases, the companies seized opportunities before their competitors, and therefore gained tremendous growth. Clearly, once AHS had installed terminals in US hospitals, it would have been difficult for others to follow suit, because no hospital manager would countenance the prospect of seven or eight companies wanting to install terminals.

The manager would however be glad if there was one
terminal through which his staff could access the
databases of all suppliers, comparing prices, availability
and delivery dates for all potential suppliers. However,
the competitiveness of US business makes that difficult to
achieve. Nevertheless, that situation is likely in due
course, making the service level of each vendor very
obvious to customers.

Timing is all important with the sort of initiative that
AHS made, and it is unlikely that any one company
would be able to repeat that experience. On the other
hand, other companies are emulating Benetton, so that
the clothing trade is becoming extremely competitive.

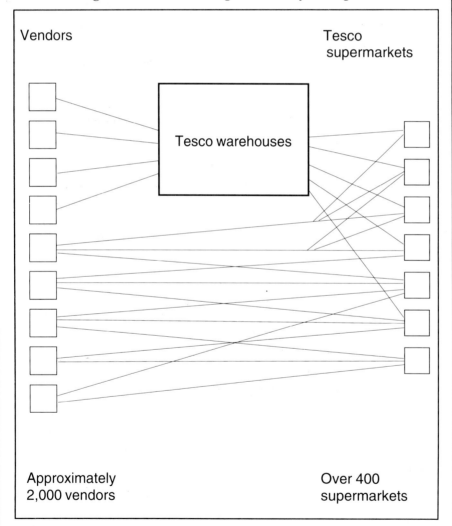

*Fig.3.1. Under Tesco's old system, most vendors received
orders from, and delivered directly to the supermarkets, with a
few supplying Tesco's warehouses*

When Benetton took up EDI, it gained considerable competitive edge; now its competitors must adopt EDI to avoid falling behind.

New ideas thrive with EDI

Toys R Us, the US toy supermarket chain combined Benetton's use of EPOS (electronic point of sale) terminals with a new idea in selling toys—in the same way that Benetton had new ideas on clothes shops. Toys R Us set up a number of toy supermarkets, and soon took 11% of the US market. It is now spreading into Europe and setting up in Japan, and in the USA has taken its marketing concept into childrens' clothes, establishing the Kids R Us supermarkets. In many other cases, EDI has been used to change the business in a progressive way.

Bigger throughput, fewer deliveries

One example of the strategy of change with EDI is that of Tesco, the company that has changed from operating supermarkets in the city centres to huge superstores on their own sites, usually on the outskirts of cities. Tesco decided to change its strategy in the early 1980s and, against the trend to distributed responsibility, it moved to centralised buying and distribution, and needed EDI to combine this approach, which promised lower overheads, greater efficiency and lower bulk prices, with a guarantee that the shelves in stores would remain stocked with goods when customers wanted them.

In 1982, 2,000 vendors supplied directly to Tesco stores, with sales representatives calling regularly on the stores' managers, and with individual stores receiving up to 50 deliveries a day, all of which could add up to pandemonium. It was decided that delivery should be centralised so that staff could concentrate on exploiting their skills and knowledge. First, purchasing was centralised, so that by 1984 sales representatives were no longer calling on the stores; instead just one from each company liaised with Tesco's head office. At about the same time, tentative moves were made towards the use of EDI, initially by the transfer of magnetic tapes by messenger from 10 big vendors, and later by leased lines.

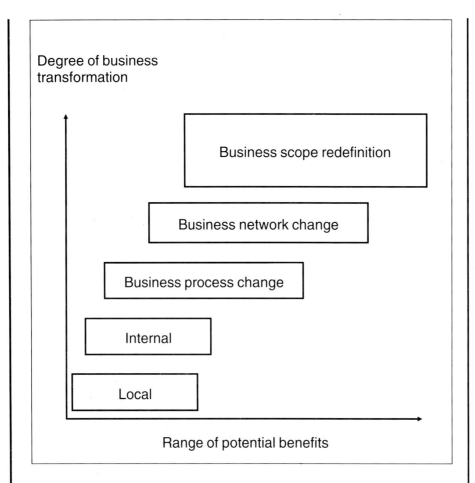

Fig. 3.2. In adopting EDI, Tesco sought to redefine the scope of its business; there is now an element of banking involved

Instead of ordering directly, the individual stores started to check stock levels with the aid of portable data capture units, and from these data, orders were fed by EDI to the Tesco head office. This led to a reduction in stock levels in the stores, and also to fresher produce. Because less space was required at the rear of each store for stock, more shelf space was made available in the store, which enabled more lines to be carried.

Centralised warehouses

To reduce the volume of traffic at individual stores, Tesco started to build a number of centralised warehouses. Initially, it set up its own depots for dry goods but relied on direct supply for goods such as bread, and on third-party warehousing for frozen and chilled goods. It was drawing goods from 22 warehouses to supply its 380 stores, which were then receiving two deliveries normally.

The centralised system led to specialisation: in the superstore, the stock controller was responsible for stocking shelves to meet demand, and was not concerned with meeting sales representatives, or placing direct orders by telephone. In the Tesco headquarters, one team of buyers was responsible for all commercial decisions, while central control was responsible for ensuring that vendors made deliveries as required, the commercial details already having been agreed. Then, the distribution centres were responsible for processing goods through to the stores in their areas as quickly as practical.

EDI integral part of system

EDI was an integral part of this new approach; it was needed to transmit orders from stores to head office, and from head office to vendors. Then, the vendors needed to inform the distribution centres of delivery times. To make the system work efficiently, many vendors needed to use EDI, and Tesco was finding the use of leased lines very complex, because a different approach was needed dependent on the make of computer and techniques used by the vendor. It therefore joined the INS Tradanet and requested its main suppliers to do likewise.

The next stage was to order and distribute fresh and frozen foods centrally. This presented particular problems because of the short lives involved. Eight composite warehouses were built on existing sites, and with the success in the information flow that EDI gave, Tesco was able to reduce the total number of warehouse sites from 22 to eight. These composite stores house foods that are frozen, chilled, and at ambient temperature. To distribute these items, Tesco uses trucks with van bodies having two movable partitions, the temperatures in the spaces being controlled to suit the produce, and of course, the volume in each section can be varied to suit the delivery.

Although almost all the main vendors transmit through Tradanet, there is an exception in the case of bread. Whereas previously, orders were placed weekly with updates 48 hours and 24 hours before each day's delivery, now they are sent directly without any forecast, and with a short lead time. Owing to the volume of business, the two biggest suppliers of bread, Allied Bakeries and British

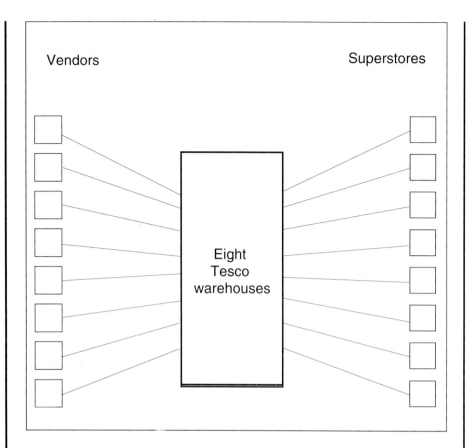

Vendors   Superstores

Eight
Tesco
warehouses

Fig. 3. 3. Some 400 vendors deliver over 90% of Tesco's goods to eight central warehouses, under EDI control

Bakeries, receive orders over leased lines, whereas Family Loaf Bakeries, William Jackson and Warburtons are connected to Tradanet. Tesco states that through the use of EDI, the stock level and wastage of bread are both reduced, while bread sales have increased.

EDI and EPOS produce new business

Overall, EDI has played a key role in increasing business at Tesco and has been instrumental in allowing the company to restructure the way in which it does business. The electronic links were extended with the introduction of Electronic Point of Sale (EPOS) terminals starting in 1987, and now extended to 178 stores. By September 1992 it is planned that EPOS will be used at all 390 stores, increasing the accuracy of the sales data transmitted to head office for faster response to trends.

Moreover, since the EPOS terminals are connected to the banks' network, it is possible for the checkout clerk to cash cheques for customers. Unlike similar services operated by most retailers—Switch is an example—in which the transactions are transmitted overnight, Tesco's superstores are on-line to the banks, so authorisation is virtually instantaneous. This service, for which Tesco charges a small fee, puts it into a completely new business, which would be impossible without EDI, and which has great potential in the future. The investment in EPOS terminals and systems alone came to £55 million, an indication of the level of investment made during the past eight years by Tesco.

Dramatic gains

The results of this investment and the gains made by EDI have been dramatic. In 1982, over 2,000 vendors supplied directly to the stores; now 93% of goods are delivered through Tesco's warehouses. Wines and spirits and many other goods have been added to the inventory as well. Despite an increase in availability of goods on the shelves in the stores, the total amount of stock held by the group has declined by no less than 50%. In addition, the lead-time has been halved with the aid of EDI.

Gains made by Tesco with EDI and centralised control		
	1982	1991
Number of products sold	5,000	16,000
Number of cases handled	50 million	400 million
Availability on shelves in stores	92%	98%
EDI vendors	None	Over 300

It is no wonder the company has grown dramatically, doubling margins and trebling profits between 1982 and 1990.

Whereas in the middle of 1989 just 2% of all Tesco's business was conducted by EDI, the broadening of the EDI base to include 300 vendors by the end of 1990 took this level up to 50%, and that includes 70% of all long-life goods. Now, some 400 vendors are trading electronically with Tesco. As a result of the use of EDI, vendors now have one document for the order, the

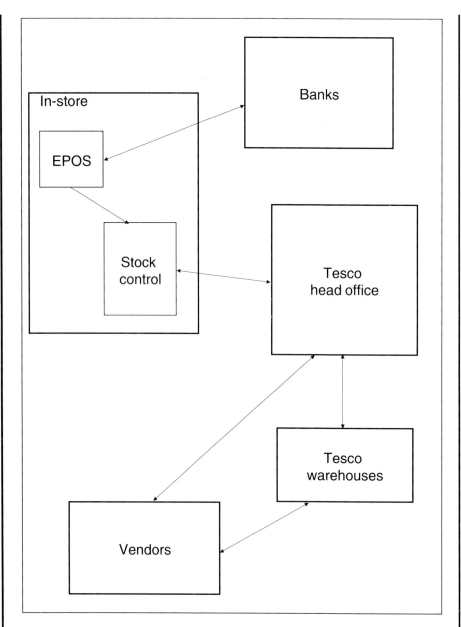

Fig. 3.4. In most Tesco superstores there are direct connections between the EPOSs and banks as well as to the in-store stock controller

despatch note, delivery note and invoice. Automatic matching of invoices to the agreed prices is being started, and the next stage is to scan all incoming goods to obtain proof of delivery. Once this system is in operation, Tesco will be able to self-bill, eliminating the need for invoices. After that will come electronic payments to complete the cycle—in the old days, with the main vendors supplying all the stores, many were sending 2,000 invoices weekly to Tesco. See Diagram 1

Unlike some hubs in an EDI community, Tesco executives do not talk about the closer business relations they have built up with their vendors. They have been concentrating on improving the service they give customers, and have used their size and growth to persuade vendors to adopt EDI. Indeed, some vendors have said that Tesco has instructed them to adopt EDI, which is in contrast to the milder tactics adopted by many companies. _ *Conor stop here*

Other chain stores, such as Littlewoods and Marks & Spencer, are users of EDI, but Littlewoods, which uses independent haulage contractors to deliver its goods, has adopted EDI principally to improve its information concerning deliveries. It has built up a community covering 75% of its supplies, the messages being confined to availability at suppliers and contract call-off of goods for delivery. Almost all its goods are delivered by two haulage contractors, and both have installed EDI links so that they can inform Littlewoods at any time exactly where the goods are, and when delivery is expected. Previously, the time from when the goods were picked up by the haulier until they were delivered was a black hole—with no one being sure whether the delivery would be made on time until the truck arrived.

EDI to reach the small man

Although a manufacturer, Birds Eye Wall's supplies retailers directly, and so its approach to EDI is close to that of a retail organisation. It adopted EDI to improve efficiency, but also found that it solved a problem that resulted from the way in which it had restructured its business to cut costs. It sends 25% of orders and receives 50% of invoices by EDI and expects the proportion of orders to reach 50% by the end of 1991. Most of its EDI business is with the large retailers, with delivery to central distribution warehouses. This sector accounts for 65% of Birds Eye Wall's business and is expected to increase to 80% before long.

At the other end of the spectrum, the company found it uneconomical to supply the small ice cream retailers directly, so it set up a chain of 42 concessionaires. Although this change improved the overall efficiency, it was a typical move by managers more interested in the overall business than the people selling their goods, and the valuable information that such retailers can give. The result was that Birds Eye Wall's found itself losing contact with developments in the trade, with the inevitably adverse effect on sales. This situation was exacerbated by the fact that the company supplied freezers for new sites, and the negotiations over this equipment tended to dominate its communications with the concessionaires.

To overcome this problem it tailored an EDI system. A software package was developed specially so that each concessionaire could collect details of daily sales together with information on changes in outlets, and new requirements for freezers. A PC with its software was installed by Birds Eye Wall's at each concessionaire, and it was connected to the IBM IN network to which Birds Eye Wall's subscribed. Now, the company receives considerable information from its concessionaires, and in turn keeps them up to date with data and messages. The result has been that despite its centralised approach, Birds Eye Wall's has regained close contact with the small retailers.

Travelling in the footsteps of the motor industry, the replacement parts distributors have started to use EDI. This followed an initiative by the Society of Motor Manufacturers and Traders (SMMT) to set up the Aftermarket Parts and Accessories Section (APAS) with a number of distributors and factors. It naturally adopted the Odette message syntax, and found that the actual form of the message was very close to that used by manufacturers, so the project could move ahead quickly. Following pilot trials, invoice and payments between the leading distributors and manufacturers have begun.

The lessons from the retail sector are that EDI cuts costs and streamlines the business. Also, it enables stock to be reduced while giving the customer greater choice—what any manufacturer wants to be able to do. Above all, however, it enables an organisation to change the way it operates, and increase sales as a result. Nor should it be forgotten that the use of EDI can improve relations with a large number of small retailers.

Chapter Four

Formula for restructuring —EDI and JIT

US auto industry cuts value of stock by $1 billion

Rover Group cuts storage space by 90%, and

Receives two-hourly deliveries in build sequence

LARGE manufacturers can use EDI to streamline the supply side or increase their ability to respond to customers. Those that supply mainly to large customers, such as Black & Decker or Rowntree Mackintosh, have used EDI to improve relations with their customers. However, most others have put the emphasis on the supply side of their business. In the future, attention will need to be given to both sides of the supply chain.

Most manufacturers that started linking EDI to their vendors did so for three reasons: first, because of their size, they have considerable influence over them, while a large volume of paperwork is involved; secondly, the networks currently available suit this type of business rather than communications with a large number of dealers. And they have a large number of small outlets for their goods each receiving a relatively small amount of paperwork.

Also, EDI became feasible as the large manufacturers in the motor and electronics industries were grappling with increased competition from Japan; they needed to cut inventories and streamline their businesses drastically—so they turned to Just-in-Time (JIT), and decided that the best way to implement the necessary controls was through EDI.

Invoices and orders

However, when manufacturers first looked at EDI, invoices and orders were the documents they considered initially. McDonnell Douglas, the US aerospace company, started using EDI for purchase orders in 1985, and by 1989 had reduced the eight weeks involved in the procurement process to just 24 hours. It has reduced inventory substantially. IBM also started with invoices and orders, and then increased the range of messages. The US motor industry has evidently been able to reduce the value of its stock by $1 billion thanks to the combination of EDI and JIT.

Savings by British Coal

British Coal, with sales of £4 billion a year, was receiving 1.75 million invoices and raising 300,000 orders when it adopted EDI. It has had a large computer network serving its distributed business for some years, and was one of the earlier manufacturers to adopt EDI enthusiastically. Its subsidiary Compower is one of the handful of software developers with considerable experience of EDI development. British Coal has some 300 EDI trading partners among its vendors, but found that since 75% of its output went to the former Central Electricity Generating Board there were limited opportunities to use EDI on the sales side. However, one area that is being developed is a system so that customers can be notified of special situations. As with all products, the quality of coal varies according to the type, and to the manner in which it has been stored. Therefore, at times, British Coal wants to sell off quickly specific quantities of coal, and this is where EDI could help.

Not that the corporation is unhappy with the gains it has made with its vendors. Messages for invoices, orders and for free text are in use, and others for order schedules, and remittance advices are now available.

To British Coal, EDI is merely an extension of its use of Information Technology (IT), but an extension with tangible benefits. It claims a saving of £50,000 a year in paperwork, and a further £30,000 attributable to the reduced number of queries that are handled.

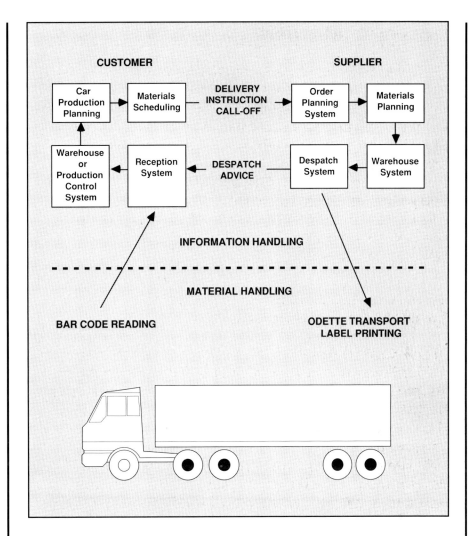

Fig. 4.1. In manufacturing, the combination of EDI, JIT and bar codes promoted by the Odette group, is a powerful method of raising efficiency

Motor industry gains

It is in the motor industry that most progress has been made in using EDI to restructure—thanks largely to the adoption of JIT delivery techniques. But more could be made with a strategic commitment to a reduction of fat in all areas and improvements in the efficiency of the total supply chain.

In the USA, General Motors (GM), Ford and Chrysler have all used EDI to implement JIT deliveries. GM has been trading electronically with many of its vendors in North America for a few years, and has recently introduced payments by EDI. This was made possible by the adoption of self-billing—what the Americans call evaluated receipts settlement—but has been held up by the fact that few banks were capable of accepting EDI messages. Now, GM is making electronic transfers through six banks, and in 1990 made 25,000 payments valued at $1 billion monthly by EDI. It has therefore cut the number of cheques issued by 44%.

Previously, a cheque took 3.6 days to reach a vendor, so when GM switched to electronic payments—the method is usually called EFT (Electronic Fund Transfer)—it decided to make payments three days later, so that the vendor would receive the funds 0.6 days earlier than formerly. Incidentally, GM calls this 'sharing' the benefits, but the 0.6 days is a mere crumb to the three days that GM gains.

In Europe, Ford is spreading EDI throughout its operations, while in the UK, construction equipment maker, J C Bamford has cut stock by 25%. But it is the Rover Group that has used EDI and JIT to restructure its manufacturing operations most dramatically.

JIT different in Japan and the West

However, JIT in Europe and the USA differs from that used in Japan. Toyota developed JIT as part of its Toyota Production System, which is intended to allow production of cars of high variety in the sequence in which they are ordered with minimum work-in-progress in the plants. These belong to the concept of lean production (See Chapter Eleven). The emphasis was, and still is, on reducing work-in-progress in the Toyota plants, but considerable effort has gone into altering the method of changing dies and tools and, in some cases, manufacture itself, to suit the concept of minimum stock and maximum variety.

At the same time, Toyota's production engineers wanted a virtual conveyor belt from the first vendor to the finished product. The Toyota Production System was a method by which Toyota changed the company culture, not just in terms of manufacture, but also in the speed with which it responded to customers' orders.

The system was taken up by other Japanese manufacturers, and not just in the motor industry. The emphasis is on making the flow of components and sub-assemblies between departments in the same plant seamless; the regular supply of small batches of components, at intervals of one or two hours, follows on from that concept.

When European and US engineers first learned of JIT, or the '*kanban*' system, they tended to look at it in relation to vendors, and in the early 1980s were saying that their vendors would not comply with such instructions. When EDI came along, they saw a way of turning JIT into a reality, at least as far as their vendors were concerned.

One reason for the emphasis placed on vendors was that in the 1970s both North American and European manufacturers had suffered chronically from labour disputes, both in their own plants and at those of vendors. The result had been frequent disruptions and chaotic stock situations. To guard against disruptions in supply, both manufacturer and vendor carried stocks to last at least a week, and most vehicle makers split orders between two or three vendors.

When there was a strike at the manufacturer, deliveries would continue to be accepted for a while in the hope that the strike would end in a couple of days. Only when it was apparent that the strike would drag on were all deliveries halted, by which time large stocks would have built up.

In addition, production control in the plants was dedicated to meeting schedules at the cost of waste. For example, to be able to supply sufficient engines for 4,000 cars a week, the plant manager might plan for 4,500, on the basis that stoppages, shortages and rejects would reduce that level to 4,000—a waste of 500 units and resources. Then, the managers of the components shops would make similar allowances, so that the schedule might call for 5,000 sets; sometimes that number would be made, at other times 4,000 and sometimes only 3,500. Since the same situation was occurring in the other departments, the whole system was out of balance, with excessive costs and poor quality the inevitable result.

Chaotic progress chasing

Whenever a strike was imminent somewhere in the industry, manufacturers found themselves fighting to obtain deliveries the next day—whatever the quality—for some components, and stopping deliveries of other components arising from excess stocks. It was said that at one time enough automatic transmissions had built up at one British manufacturer to last for a year. This poor control allowed vendors to deliver and invoice for an extra truck load of components because they thought that a stoppage would hurt their cashflow the following month.

Gradually, this system was improved, but even in 1980, when the Rover Group plant at Longbridge was laid out for the Metro, there was a special buffer store in the body shop to hold a substantial buffer stock of body panels, which was in addition to those in various storage areas in the plant.

Revolution at Rover

Clearly, to move from that situation to one in which the stock level held at the side of the line will last for just two hours calls for little short of a revolution in thinking by both managers and the workforce, but that is what the Rover Group has achieved—and EDI has most certainly been the enabling technology.

The combination of EDI and JIT was seen as a way of improving efficiency and quality to match the Japanese. As in other industries, purchase orders and delivery instructions—sometimes termed call-off instructions—received priority, and soon the manufacturers found that the purchasing department could concentrate on negotiating contracts and prices and finding new products—the routine of raising purchase orders to arrange deliveries of components for which terms had been agreed was largely automated.

The Rover Group first became interested in EDI in the early 1980s, and joined other members of the UK Society of Motor Manufacturers and Traders (SMMT) to establish standards for EDI in the motor industry in 1984, and the result was the Odette standard, now used by 800

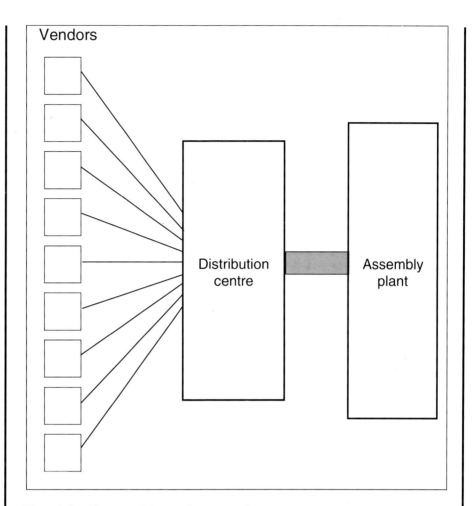

Fig. 4.2. About 100 vendors supply components once or twice a week to the Rover Group's distribution centre near Longbridge, from which the company draws stock every two hours

companies in the industry in Europe. An industry standard was particularly important in the European motor sector because a number of large vendors supply several of the large manufacturers. Had each vehicle manufacturer adopted its own system, vendors would have been faced with the need to purchase different computers and software. The situation would have been aggravated by the fact that JIT means a slightly different thing to each car manufacturer. As it is, several component suppliers in the UK have had to install different systems alongside one another to meet the requirements of three or four competing customers: Ford, GM, Nissan and Rover Group.

Although the aim was for a pan-European standard, some German manufacturers had started developing a standard in parallel with the SMMT, and so they still use a VDA format, but also are involved in the Odette group. In the future, only Odette messages are to be promoted in Germany, however.

Invoices overtaken by JIT

Rover started using EDI almost as soon as the networks began operating in the UK in 1985, and since AT&T Istel had started life as Rover Group's systems department, it was natural that it would use AT&T Istel's AT&T EDI network, which is used widely in the motor industry. Rover started with invoices, and then devised its own JIT system to operate with EDI messages—the Minimum Inventory Concept (MIC).

In fact, Rover was inspired to take up the idea wholeheartedly to solve particular problems. From 1986, assembly at the Cowley plant in Oxford was to be carried out in a number of inter-connected buildings making access for vendors' vehicles difficult. In 1989 it was decided that if space was to be found for a new assembly line for the Rover 200 and 400 models at Longbridge, Birmingham, the huge goods inwards store and receiving deck in the Metro plant had to go—leading to a reduction in storage space of at least 90%.

In both cases Rover decided the solution was to build distribution centres outside the plants but which vendors would stock. Operated by an independent transport company—BRS at Cowley, and TNT at Longbridge—the distribution centres contain stock maintained at specified levels by the 100-odd vendors. From the point of view of accounting, until components are drawn by Rover from the distribution centre, the components remain the property of the vendor.

Although the stock in the distribution centre at Cowley is enough for five days' production, space at Longbridge is sufficient only for two or three days' production, and in both cases the space is strictly limited—there is no room for extra components to meet 'if or but' situations.

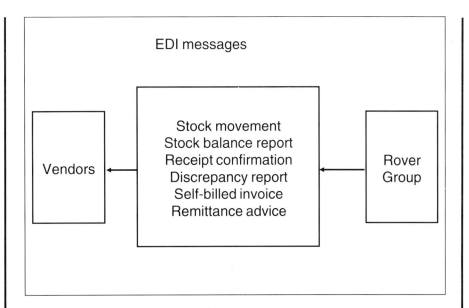

Fig. 4.3. Rover Group's EDI messages were developed specifically to facilitate JIT deliveries

Standard pallets

In line with the JIT concept, pallets (all in a range of standard sizes) are drawn from the distribution centre and ferried to the line in lots sufficient for an average of two hours' production. Normally, just two pallets are kept at the side of the line, and only when one is empty can another one be obtained. Therefore, the actual amount of vendors' stock in the plant is similar to that carried in Japanese plants. As yet, the same control has not been exercised over components and assemblies produced in the Rover plants, however.

For this system to operate efficiently, Rover had to be able to notify vendors immediately it withdrew components from the centre, and this is where EDI came in; without it, the information would have reached the vendor too late for the system to work. Rover devised a number of EDI messages in the Odette format for:

☐ Warehouse stock balance report;
☐ Stock movement report;
☐ Confirmation of receipt of goods;
☐ Discrepancy advice, for when the actual goods do not match those advised;
☐ Pre-notification of the impending delivery of goods— this message is sent by the vendor to the Rover Group.

When the parts are withdrawn from the distribution centre, Rover accepts delivery in the technical sense, and immediately sends delivery confirmation to the vendor. Because the components are supplied in specially-formed pallets, it is easy for Rover to check the accuracy of delivery. Therefore, once this system was instituted, Rover started to raise self-billing invoices, and these now account for a substantial proportion of the approximately one million invoices the company used to receive annually. It also eliminated many of the invoices that had been transferred to EDI.

Previous to the use of EDI, it took six-to-eight weeks for the invoice to be received and validated, simply because Rover did not have sufficient confidence in the accuracy of delivery documentation to self-bill.

Sequenced delivery and storage

Storage in the distribution centre is suitable only for components in which there are few variations, such as heaters, starter motors and windscreen wiper motors. Components of which there are many different versions are delivered directly to the assembly line—generally in two-hourly batches—and in sequence. In other words, if the schedule calls for a white car to be followed by a green one and a red one, then the trim panels are supplied in the pallet in that order, so the operator just

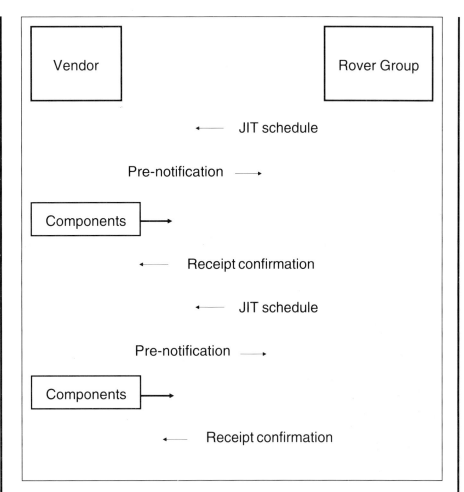

Fig. 4.4. Components sent directly by the vendor to the assembly line are controlled by a special set of messages, including the Syncro message for sequenced deliveries

picks them out of the pallet sequentially, without wasting time selecting the correct colour and grade. Clearly, this system requires considerable organisation, but contributes to efficient assembly.

When the completed body-in-white emerges from the body shop, the specification is fixed. There are then some 13 hours before it reaches final assembly as it passes through the paint shop and finishing operations. From this point, Rover decides the specification of each car by matching the situation with orders.

Rover will have sent the fortnightly schedule the previous Friday for the current week, and now needs to update that. To collate all the data Rover needs four hours, and then distributes the updated fortnightly schedule to the vendors, giving them instructions on what components to send for each block of two hours of production.

Lots for two hours' production

For example, in the case of Rover 200/400 door trim panels, of which there are 160 variants, the vendor will receive notification of the sequence of build a few hours before the panels are required. It must then pack panels in the pallets in the order in which they will be used and deliver them to the line, with a maximum lead time of eight hours. At least one hour is required for loading, delivery and unloading, and in some cases two hours—however none of the vendors of these components is more than one and a half hours from the Longbridge plant. To save time, all components involved in this sequenced deliveries are supplied in wheeled trolleys.

Such a system would have been considered totally unacceptable only a decade ago, and would be impractical without EDI. Indeed, a special Odette message called Syncro was developed for sequenced deliveries; it allows the sequence of packing to be specified.

To match the short lead times, some companies have set up local satellite plants in the Japanese manner to cope. One is TRW, which supplies steering gears from its Resolven and Clevedon plants to its Frankley depot, and then carries out final assembly as it receives delivery instructions from Rover.

Techniques adopted for the Rover 200/400 and 800 series have yet to be extended to other product lines. For example, because the Metro plant was planned in the days when guarding against stoppages was considered essential, there is a stock of 300 painted Metro bodies at the beginning of the assembly line. Therefore, lead time is insufficient for sequential deliveries to be used on that model.

Rover's storage area cut by 90%

The proof of Rover's success is in its distribution centres: in 1986 one was built at Cowley with space for five days' components from major vendors; the centre for the Rover 200/400 at Longbridge has space for just two days' stock, representing a reduction in reserve stocks—for this is what these centres are—of 60%. Moreover, the space for storage in the assembly plant at Longbridge has been cut by 90%. Now, MIC is being adopted in departments in Rover plants, such as in the body-in-white shop. Also, Land-Rover is following Rover's lead into EDI.

Ford builds own network

Over the past four years, Ford has converted its main vendors to the use of EDI for some messages, and is now accepting advance shipping notes by EDI from a number of vendors. Although Ford has used EDI to implement JIT, it does not quantify the benefits of either concept, considering these are merely two of the many tools helping Ford to remain competitive.

Ford took a different approach from its competitors (other than GM) in that it set up its own network—Fordnet—and supplied vendors with its own software for use on IBM mainframes, minicomputers or PCs. Thus, the vendor only had to buy a PC and modem, or use its existing machines. Since there is no subscription fee for a network, Ford was able to convert quickly a large number of vendors to EDI. It identified initially 200 key vendors in the UK and 200 in Germany, and now virtually all of these use EDI. Each vendor supplies significant amounts in both volume and value.

Ford has incorporated Fordnets in the IBM mainframe systems in the UK, Germany and Spain. Initially, the material release, a weekly schedule stretching forward six months, was converted to EDI, and is not now sent in paper form at all. Next came the daily call-off, which Ford places in the electronic mailboxes in Fordnet each night. Vendors call in the following morning, and deliver the goods that afternoon—some vendors deliver four times a day as part of Ford's approach to JIT.

All Ford EDI messages are in the German VDA format, largely because at the time when it started Ford found more vendors using them—an indication that German vendors already supplying German car companies were more advanced in the use of EDI than their British counterparts at that time. However, Ford does use the Odette label, although at present it sees little value in the use of the bar codes—it wants one of its employees to verify that the goods have actually been received. One reason for this is that Ford is operating a self-billing system for most components and this is actioned on verification of delivery.

Although bar codes are only just coming into use on pallets entering from outside, some are used in-house to indicate part numbers and quantity. Ford sees the indication of routing of pallets inside its plants as the best use of bar codes.

Also involved in the system are the main haulage contractors, such as BRS, which indicate to Ford when a consignment leaves a depot, and where relevant when it arrives at a ferry terminal. Ford is expanding its use of EDI:

☐ To receive quotations and sample results from vendors;
☐ To send orders and quality performance data to vendors;
☐ For vendors to send information regarding material availability to the haulage contractor.

Swedes follow Odette trail

In Sweden, the four manufacturers—Volvo Car, Volvo Truck, Saab Automobile and Scania—have used EDI since 1989 to cut the lead time of components supplied by vendors by two to five days. This is estimated to have saved the industry at least 280 million Swedish krona. In addition, larger vendors admit to the use of EDI having a payback period of between only 3-18 months.

As a group, the Swedish industry adopted Odette message standards and the Odette label for pallets, which includes bar codes. By May 1991, 241 vendors were using EDI for some messages, with all those vendors receiving delivery schedules electronically. Of these, 142 are sending their despatch advice notes by EDI, but only one is receiving the Syncro message, in which components are called off in the sequence in which they will be used in the plant. These components are delivered to a tight JIT schedule. Significantly, 291 companies have adopted the Odette label for their pallets, 50 in advance of using EDI.

With the combination of JIT and EDI, the vehicle industry has raised efficiency, and in some cases made dramatic changes to its relationship with vendors. That process is continuing, but there is also a need to put some emphasis on improving relations with the dealers and customers.

In fact, GM has started to do just this in its Saturn Corporation. Unusually, the network is based on a satellite system, which is generally preferred for sending data from one to many points. Nevertheless, the same system is used for both vendors and dealers. When GM sends an order to a vendor by EDI it is sent in such a way that a bar-coded shipping label can be generated. This label is attached to the pallet sent to the GM plant, where it is scanned and the data fed into the financial and materials control system. When the components or materials are drawn from the stores, a liability is entered in the payments system, and payment is made automatically by EFT.

Unusually, Saturn manages the dealers' inventory. When parts are required, the order is recognised by Saturn, which sends the order to the component supplier. Warranty claims and data relating to the sales of cars to dealers are transmitted by the same system; Saturn sends only one piece of paper to dealers—the Manufacturer's Statement of Origin, required to meet US Federal law.

In terms of EDI, Saturn is leading the way to completely paperless trading, and the opportunity of improving relations through the whole supply chain from materials vendor to the customer.

Chapter Five

Reaching world class in electronics

EDI one of four planks of strategy

Vendors' lead time down from 80 to 40 days

Inventory cut from £15 million to £5 million

TO ACHIEVE world-class performance, manufacturers
need to upgrade all aspects of their operations, from
the ordering of the raw materials through to delivery of
the product and after-sales service. Any manufacturer
that picks up Just-in-Time (JIT), EDI or installs a dozen
robots without tackling the other aspects of its business
will not achieve world-class standards; the
newly-installed efficient sector of the business will be
dragged down into the morass of inefficiency by waste
elsewhere, and by the attitude of people who see
themselves surrounded by inefficiency.

EDI is an integral part of any upgrading process, but is
lost without attention to other strategies either
beforehand, or at the same time. One company that
recognised this situation is Mitel Manufacturing
Technologies, the manufacturing arm of Mitel
Telecommunications. Owned 51% by BT (formerly
British Telecom), Mitel manufactures in the UK and
North America, but the UK operations took the lead
when it came to EDI.

In the late 1980s, Mitel's situation was typical of
companies making a wide variety of electronics
assemblies, in its case digital telephone exchanges for

both private networks—from a few lines upward—and for large switches for the public telecommunications authorities. Although the number of assemblies and components in electronics assemblies are fewer than in a passenger car, variety is very high, with the larger units being tailored to suit the customer's requirement. Therefore, inventory tends to be high, while the small size of electronics components leads to high stock levels in the assembly plants. The situation had been aggravated as extra models were added in an effort to meet customers' demands.

When Mitel decided to raise its standards and move toward lean production, it decided to adopt four strategies. These were:

- ☐ To implement the Cosby system of total quality control (TQC);
- ☐ To make some changes in the company that would produce visible results;
- ☐ To improve supplier relationship with the aid of JIT;
- ☐ To adopt EDI.

Mitel did not consider the combination of JIT and EDI sufficient; its managers recognised that to make worthwhile improvements to performance, they had to involve all employees in the programme.

Inside the plants, Mitel adopted cells for manufacture since this approach lends itself to low volumes, and generally gives a higher overall operating efficiency than one continuous line. It also tends to improve the morale of operators. To change the attitude of its workforce, Mitel replaced the conventional maintenance department with fewer specialists, and introduced a system of planned maintenance to be carried out by the operators of the machines themselves. This approach reduced downtime, and increased the interest of the operators in their machines.

Kanban inside the plant, JIT for vendors

Significantly, unlike many manufacturers, Mitel did not merely inflict JIT schedules on its suppliers, but also introduced a *kanban* system in its own plants so that stock could be produced only when the following section ran short—the classic Japanese pull system. Only when this was operating did Mitel consider it realistic to introduce JIT deliveries from vendors. This approach brings greater benefits than receiving deliveries from vendors only to a JIT schedule, and is essential for any company that is intent on becoming a lean manufacturer.

Mitel started its upgrading programme in 1988, and EDI was introduced only after many changes had been made. With all four strategies, Mitel has:

☐ Reduced the value of its inventory from £15 million to £5 million over the past three years;
☐ Reduced work-in-progress from £5 million to £800,000;
☐ Cut the lead time for its products from 58 to five days;
☐ Cut the defects levels from 20 to 0.2 defects/system.

A target of zero defects is part of the drive to quality, and came from the Cosby system. It has proved highly successful, with the peer pressure of employees on those producing defective components to improve being very strong.

EDI has come into play in reducing lead-time of components and sub-assemblies from vendors. 'EDI took 10 days out of the lead time for free,' observed an executive. Previously, Mitel had to allow 10 days for the postal delivery of the purchase orders and acceptance. Now, they are transmitted and acceptance confirmed in the same day.

In 1987, the lead time for 80% of components from Mitel's vendors was within 80 days, which was typical for European companies. Mitel cut that to 70 days immediately it introduced EDI, and with other improvements the lead times of 66% of components were brought down to 40 days, and almost all the rest down to 60 days by 1989.

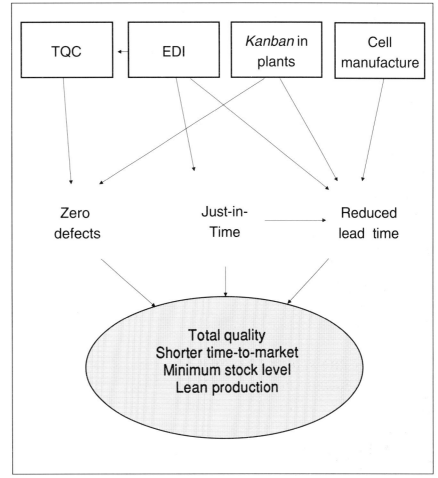

Fig. 5.1. If incorporated into a manufacturing strategy, EDI can contribute to the attainment of world-class levels with lean production

Now, Mitel is aiming to reduce the lead time to 25 days for all vendors, and expects to achieve that, largely through the use of EDI to update long-term schedules and to call off deliveries as needed. Although the first 10 days comes easily with EDI, remaining improvements depend on the reliability of the information the customer can give the vendor about future production, and the trust the vendor puts in that data. In the 1970s, vendors would not have acted on such information from their customers; they were too used to attending scheduling meetings where the computer print-out of the schedule ended up as a mass of handwritten figures that bore no resemblance to the original. Efforts to raise efficiency to compete with the Japanese have led to better scheduling by European manufacturers, but improvements of the magnitude made by Mitel depend on trust—and EDI fosters that trust.

To handle its EDI transmissions, Mitel adopted the INS Tradanet network, and claims that the payback period amounted to 10 months from the time it started to trade electronically with 30 vendors.

It has also started to make payments by EDI, which saves half a day's time of a senior executive, and eliminates the delay while he finds that time. Administration generally is reduced, and again, trust is increased.

Mitel started transmitting orders electronically first—because that gave the biggest strategic gain—and is following with the acceptance of invoices and the transmission of remittance advice. However, it is switching to self-billing where practical, and in that case it gives the vendor the right to audit stock levels of its components.

Act of faith by computer makers

Several other electronics companies have adopted EDI, although as might be expected, makers of computers have adopted EDI almost as an act of faith.

IBM operates its own network, and so has adopted EDI for transactions both within its own organisation and with its suppliers. It now has over 600 EDI connections in 20 countries, and because of the size of the operations, it designates one plant as the controller for deliveries from each supplier. It expects to trade electronically with 2,000 vendors by 1992; the company was expecting to save $60 million in the period 1988-92. It started with purchase orders, and in Europe well over 80% are now sent by EDI.

IBM's approach was typical of that of the multinational computer and electronics companies. It started its EDI project in 1987 and adopted its own IBM Information Network (IN). It now has over 400 EDI trading partners. There are 11 IBM plants in six countries in Europe, and IBM has adopted a policy of concentrating all EDI transactions with each vendor through one of its plants. With its large network of product design offices, production engineering departments and plants, IBM also developed an internal EDI system, which now makes 20,000 business transactions weekly. The messages in use are:

☐ Purchase order;
☐ Response to purchase order;
☐ Change to purchase order;
☐ Despatch advice;
☐ JIT control;
☐ Invoice.

The company expects the transfer of Computer Aided Design (CAD) data to and from vendors to bring most benefits; but is not near doing that on a routine basis, not least because only after various divisions had spent a considerable amount of effort on different CAD systems did the company standardise packages.

In Scandinavia, IBM also uses EDI to expedite the delivery of PCs. Delivery of PS/2 products has been centralised at Taastrup in Denmark, and EDI was considered indispensible in reducing delivery times, without increasing stock levels. However, at first the time required by Danish Customs to clear shipments by ferry to Norway was holding up deliveries. This delay was eliminated when IBM became the first company to deal with Danish Customs through EDI; indeed, deliveries to Norway are cleared by customs over the EDI network in 10 minutes.

Since IBM sends advance information by EDI to the ferry operator, DFDS, the schedule can be arranged very quickly. Also, there is just one page of documentation against 50 required previously. DFDS found that whereas it required one person to work full-time on the paperwork for IBM deliveries, now he spends only five minutes daily doing the same work.

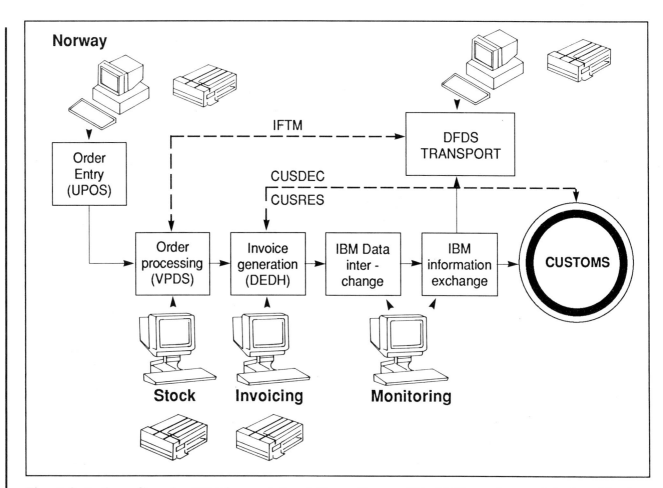

Fig. 5.2. In Scandinavia, IBM has cut the delivery times of its PS/2 products with the aid of EDI, which is used even to clear Customs

Cutting the order cycle

To prepare for what they perceive as the future of EDI, both Digital Equipment and Hewlett Packard operate X.400 networks (See Chapter Seven) between their plants and offices in Europe. ICL sends over 30% of its purchase orders by EDI, and as a result has cut the cycle from order to acknowledgement from 20 to three days. It also books 80% of air freight movements by EDI.

NCR and Apple Computer are also EDI users, and in both cases the initial emphasis was placed on purchase orders. At first, Apple found that to use EDI it needed to change its purchasing system, and this reflects the experience of other users. Indeed, Kodak found that 90% of the work involved in adopting EDI was in making such changes. NCR has concentrated on cutting inventory levels, and calls off deliveries at just 48 hours' notice.

Black and Decker was one of many companies persuaded by the large retailers to use EDI and it trades electronically with a number of them, and with 40 of its vendors. Invoices received electronically account for 70% of its expenditure in the UK, and it is expanding the system to Europe. However, Black & Decker has found the going slow because of the relative lack of use of EDI on the Continent. The company wants to exchange CAD data with its vendors so that operations can be co-ordinated further. It is also in the process of planning the automation of data handling for both purchasing and manufacture.

JIT for dyeing and finishing

An interesting application in the textile industry reflects the early work of Benetton: Coats Viyella has devised a system that automates messages related to the dyeing and finishing of garments and rolls of material in order to cut lead time. The largest textile group in Europe, Coats Viyella has 16 dyeing and finishing plants in the group. It has been using EDI to process the call-off orders from large retailers for some time, and in expanding the use of EDI wanted to develop a new system that would not just streamline one operation, but that could be used elsewhere in the group.

Dyeing and finishing can take place at one of three stages: on raw yarn; after spinning; or when the garment is complete. The choice of the stage depends on the product. It is a critical path in the process, and is performed two or three times in the production process for some products. In the case of garments, each lot consists of 30 packs of 12, and 40 lots are transferred daily from knitting to the dyeing/finishing plant.

Owing to the variety involved, the dyeing bill which accompanied each lot was a complex piece of paper. It combined:

- ☐ Advice note;
- ☐ Details of the lot number and date;
- ☐ Quality of finish;
- ☐ Style;
- ☐ Construction of garment;
- ☐ Colouring details.

With a long-term objective in view, Coats Viyella decided to use a VAN rather than direct lines for transmissions, and then found that it was necessary to devise its own message, because it did not expect any other companies would wish to use it. In the event, it was able to devise such a message, incorporating the standard leader and segment of the Tradacoms message, and was able to define all the parameters that the plants required.

Used in fabrics division as well

Now, EDI messages are sent instead of the paperwork, and as a result, the group has saved 20 hours/week of keying in of data. In addition, lead-time has been cut by half a day, which is significant in the fast-moving retail business.

Because Coats Viyella adopted a comprehensive message format, it has been able to expand its use to the fabric division, and it is now being adopted for transactions in the hosiery division.

Whereas most of these manufacturers have concentrated on the supply side, Wavin Building Products, which makes plastic pipes, guttering and drains for the building trade, decided to adopt EDI to improve efficiency and speed up its response to its customers.

Graham Builders Merchants and Jewsons account for 40% of its business, and it also supplies companies such as W H Smith Do-it-All and Texas Homecare, which are using EDI. It now transmits all invoices to Grahams and Jewsons by EDI; orders to W H Smith Do-it-All; and invoices, orders and credit notes to Texas Homecare.

Mixing EDI and telephone order-taking

One of its problems was that it had established an efficient order entry system under which customers could telephone orders for instant keying-in by the operators. This is still used for a substantial amount of the business, and the company had to devise a means of entering EDI orders, without shutting down the telephone ordering system. It has adopted an asynchronous system that allows EDI orders to be interspersed with telephone orders.

One big advantage is that in the EDI file there is actually one line for each item ordered, whereas a conventional order might have 20 or 30 items on an order. Quite often a few of the items, or a small quantity of one item would not be available, which presented problems in matching invoices and orders. With EDI, one invoice can be sent for a portion of the order, and another to match up with items sent later.

Because Wavin's products are light but bulky, it has tailored a system of loading vehicles and delivering the goods—for example, it provides the driver with a route map for every journey, so that arrival times can be guaranteed within 20 minutes of the expected time. Therefore, it can inform customers by EDI of the delivery time so that a forklift truck can be ready for the arrival of the vehicle. The driver does not need to wait around for a forklift truck to be found, so EDI saves here as well.

With the use of 2,000 different packages for its products each year, Rowntree Mackintosh adopted EDI to tailor the information related to each batch of products, and to produce order where chaos could reign previously. It adopted bar codes for its products, and for the materials from vendors. It has been receiving orders and sending invoices to the main retail groups by EDI for some time, and is now moving toward weekly and monthly forecasts. Reflecting its position as a supplier to large retailers, Rowntree Mackintosh's purchasing side is less advanced; so far, it is sending call-off orders to two or three engineering suppliers only.

From operational to strategic gains

Most manufacturing companies that have adopted EDI did so for fairly routine purposes at first. But once they had the system up and running, managers found that there were more exciting applications. In many cases, EDI has been vital in rejuvenating a company, and in others has led to much better relations being established between trading partners. Criticisms are made of the slow progress in the development of industry-wide messages for other purposes than replacing paper invoices and orders, but as shown by Rover and Coats Viyella, special messages can be produced and used quite easily.

More significant, though, is the fact that EDI can allow companies to manage their businesses in ways that are not practical without it.

Chapter Six

Networks for EDI

Networks fill the void between trading partners

Offer wide services to manufacturers

But public data networks compete for business

ONCE the decision to adopt EDI has been taken the method of communication between partners needs to be decided. In Britain, the choice is one of leased lines between partners or the use of a VAN (Value-added network) as an intermediary. However, in France and Germany only 10% of EDI traffic is handled by VANs, the remainder being transmitted over the public data network (PDN). Although PDNs are likely to be used more in future in the UK, the VANs compensate for the higher cost with a more resilient user-orientated service.

At present, the choice is between a VAN or leased line; if there is considerable traffic, requiring rapid response between two partners only, the leased line would be the first choice, but in most other cases, the VANs are much more attractive.

It was not uncommon in the early days of EDI for trials to be held between a customer and five to 10 vendors over leased lines. Tesco is one company that opted for that route, but once it had established a system of operation, it chose to use a VAN wherever practical. The disadvantages with the leased lines were that two to four months were required before they could be installed, and owing to the different makes of computers and types of software in use by vendors, the support required was found to be greater than could be provided effectively.

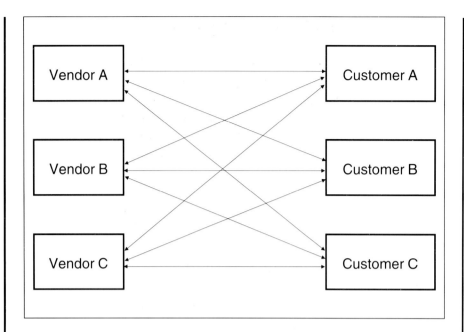

Fig. 6.1. Companies can be connected directly through the telephone lines or the public data network

Moreover, if the throughput is substantial, it is normal to use two lines to guard against failure, which increases the costs.

Tesco did retain leased lines for some big vendors for some time, but has now switched to high-speed leased lines that connect directly to INS's Tradanet. These operate at 64 kbit/s—that allows transmission of 25 Mbytes data hourly.

An advantage of the use of a VAN is that messages can be sent to several partners or downloaded from a number of partners in one session, thus reducing communications time. Also, any worthwhile VAN offers a 365 day, 24 hour service, so that trading partners do not need to be in the same time zone, or even work the same hours. In addition, proven software suitable for the VANs is available.

VAN for a trading community

What sort of VAN is used for EDI communications? It consists of a network of communications lines emanating from a central computer complex. The central computer controls the system, store messages in customers' mailboxes, keeps back-up files, audits transactions, and carries out translation. In the telecommunications network itself are access points near the main business centres.

The VAN ensures that all messages are received, stored and forwarded in their entirety without corruption, whereas users of direct links to partners need to check for errors themselves. The VAN also holds a back-up copy of the message to guard against hardware failure.

As for the time element, INS claims that so long as no format translation is required, transmission is instantaneous. AT&T Istel guarantees to process 98% of data not requiring format translation within 15 minutes, and to process all such data within 90 minutes. Where translation is required, 98% of data are processed within 30 minutes, and all data within 90 minutes. The messages are filed chronologically.

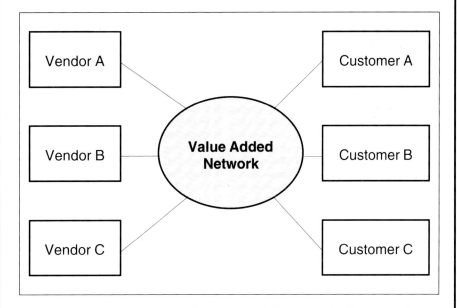

Fig. 6.2. A VAN can handle many of the technicalities in the connections between a large group of trading partners

Where several delivery instructions are required each day, the recipient needs to call up the network at hourly intervals, although it is possible for the network to inform the computer handling EDI data that there is a message awaiting collection. There is no need for regular calls to be made to the VAN, thus automating the system further.

The VAN consists of several different elements, but it is the service that sets it apart from other systems. Typical is AT&T Istel's network, now called AT&T EDI, which consists of:

☐ Infotrac communications network;
☐ The interchange centre at Redditch for receipt of transmissions, securing against loss, validation, format translation where required, and delivery to the mailbox;
☐ Support team and help desk.

There are three main VANs operating in the UK, but several more will be available by 1992-3. The existing VANs are:

☐ INS's Tradanet;
☐ AT&T Istel's AT&T EDI;
☐ IBM's Information Network.

There are also a number of smaller specialised VANs. INS is the largest of the three major VANs, with over 60% of the UK market, and 38% of the European market, according to Input, a market research organisation.

Ford and GM both use their own networks, and in Europe Ford set up Fordnets in the IBM mainframe systems in the UK, Germany and Spain. Each vendor is issued with software, and since Ford bears the cost of the network and software, the cost to the vendor is much lower than if a VAN had been used.

VAN services

Each VAN operates a similar service, with storage in mailboxes, logging of calls, software and support services. The choice of a VAN is usually determined as much by the existing EDI communities as by the services offered. Since January 1990, there has been a link between INS and AT&T Istel, while IBM is planning such a link. Eventually, the links between networks need to be as seamless as that between the telephone companies in different countries.

To date, such links are not as simple as they might be. For example, although the Danish network Dannet was able to negotiate an agreement with the Swedish and Norwegian networks for there to be no billing when a message was transferred from one network to another, it was unable to do so with the international networks.

INS Tradanet owes its size to its use by the bulk of the retailers—nine of the top 10—and their vendors. Key users in the retail sector include Asda, B&Q, Boots Company, Marks & Spencer, Sainsburys and Tesco. These companies have built up EDI communities with their vendors, and some have more than 400 EDI partners. However, Tradanet is not used only by retailers and their vendors. Included in the users which number over 3,000—up from 2,200 in twelve months— are:

- ☐ Chemical and pharmaceutical companies such as BASF, BDH, Ciba Geigy, Glaxo, six ICI companies, Johnson & Johnson, and Rhone-Poulenc;
- ☐ Electronics companies including BICC Cables, Cossor Electronics, Digital Equipment, Fujitsu Microelectronics, GEC Plessey Telecoms, Honeywell, Intel, Mitel, Mitsubishi Electric UK, Motorola, Rank Xerox and STC Telecommunications;
- ☐ Many oil and gas companies;
- ☐ International transport companies and forwarders.

Among the recent groups to use Tradanet are forwarding agents and shippers, whose Ediship is designed for international operation, allowing a forwarding agent to discover which shipper best meets its requirements for each consignment. Thus, the whole process of international transport will become more efficient.

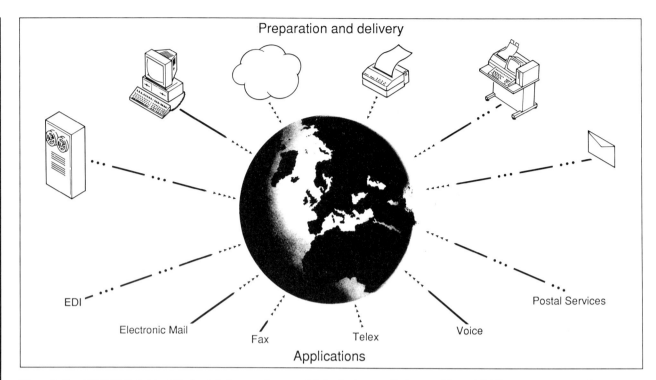

Fig. 6.3. AT&T Istel's Global Messaging, which is intended to allow EDI messages to be output in any form in the main industrial nations of the world

Although Tradacoms, the message format used mainly by the retail industry, was the main format supported by Tradanet initially, users can send messages in Odette or Edifact formats, so it is a multiple-message VAN. Indeed, the choice of a particular VAN does not limit the type of message that can be used; generally, any format can be used. (See Chapter Seven for message formats).

Motor industry standard

AT&T Istel built its network around the motor industry following the Odette initiative to establish standard messages and formats for that industry. However, it is also used by a large number of engineering companies, and includes British Coal and British Rail among its users.

IBM concentrated initially on building up a network of its own suppliers—Texas Instruments was the first user—but is also involved in several other areas. For example, V.A.G. (United Kingdom) uses the IBM Information Network to link Volkswagen, Audi and MAN dealers with its head office at Milton Keynes.

Although AT&T Istel derives a substantial amount of business from manufacturing industry, it also supports a number of other communities.

Scrutinise list of users

Obviously, any company coming into EDI should scrutinise the lists of users of these networks to ascertain which one its potential trading partners are using. The costs involved, discussed in Chapter Thirteen, differ considerably, and so should be investigated. The company should also discuss the matter with its main partners. There are many pitfalls; one company that had built up its EDI operations to supply its goods to big retailers assumed that it would use Tradanet for EDI to its vendors. It soon found that nearly all of them were using AT&T EDI, and had to join that as well.

Two other considerations in the selection of a VAN are whether any international links are required, and the protocols and message formats involved. EDI is now becoming feasible internationally on a routine basis, although most British companies will find fewer foreign partners already using EDI than in the UK.

IBM established its Information Network for international use from the start, while INS is connected to the global network operated by GEIS, which owns INS jointly with ICL. In 1990, AT&T Istel launched a new company, Global Message Services (GMS) to combine the AT&T Istel network services with AT&T's worldwide network, which has major nodes in the USA, UK and Japan.

In September 1991, it merged its Edict service with AT&T EDI, which had been developed in the USA, and so now offers the features of Edict with those of AT&T EDI. Therefore, X.400 gateways are available. Included in the services of GMS are:

☐ AT&T EDI;
☐ AT&T Mail, an electronic mail service;
☐ Enhanced facsimile service, which combines store-and-forward capability with output in fax form.

The trend in EDI is for such services to be integrated. For example, BT's EDI*Net, expected to be available in 1992, is part of a worldwide system, Global Network Service.

Satellite service

All the European networks are based on terrestrial lines, but BAe plans to launch a VAN service based on a combination of terrestrial and satellite channels. The idea is to offer a full service, with the satellite being used principally for the movement of bulk data from one point to many points—as in the case of one manufacturer to many distributors, or a head office to its regional offices or supermarkets.

In addition, large companies that use EDI almost continually to control deliveries will need a back-up to keep transmissions going should there be faults on telephone lines. At present, the only alternative is a telephone or leased line at another site. Satellite or microwave lines are the natural alternatives.

In fact, on one occasion, the Brentwood telephone exchange was out of order for almost two days, shutting down Ford's British EDI operations. Ford had to rely on vendors telephoning to an office at another site for information on deliveries. Clearly, a back-up is needed, and either a direct microwave link, or a satellite service is the answer.

There is, however, one major problem with satellite services in Europe, and this is that currently they are operated by Eutelstat, which in turn is owned by the European telephone companies. Naturally, this cartel does not want competition, so the price of satellite communications is high. Leading the challenge to Eutelstat, however, is Microspace, a company that has been set up to broadcast data to European countries other than France, where the nationalised monopoly prevents it from operating. The use of monopolistic power to prevent competition is clearly against the trend both in telecommunications and in the EC generally, and cannot be expected to survive.

Common carriers enter the fray

Ironically, despite the situation with satellites, the telecommunications common carriers, such as BT, are now making a determined effort to offer EDI over the normal telephone lines. Once the Integrated Services Digital Network (ISDN) is generally available—likely by 1995—the common carriers will be in a better position to offer such a service, since an ISDN phone line has two channels each with a 64kbit/s transmission rate, making very fast data transfers practical.

The combination of ISDN and a store-and-forward facility should provide an inexpensive alternative to the use of a VAN, and will clearly increase the use of EDI dramatically. However, ISDN is feasible only as a carrier

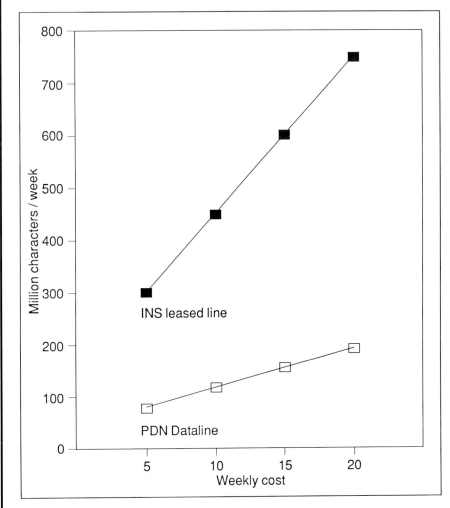

Fig. 6.4. The cost of the public data network is significantly lower than that of a 9.6kbit/s leased line to a network but does not include services such as management and security

of data if the sender and receiver are both using it. Therefore, users may still prefer to use a VAN; INS for one intends to support ISDN links to its VAN as soon as demand is there.

The packet switched system used already in the PDNs has a store-and-forward capability, and it is this that is being used instead of VANs on the Continent. Data are sent over a normal telephone line to the nearest PDN gateway—usually a local call—and then stored prior to being sent over ultra-high speed lines to another gateway, and thence to the recipient's mailbox. Such PDNs are used for both national and international transmissions.

Scandinavians opt for direct links

Because of its store-and-forward capability, essential for the operation of packet switching, the PDN is a powerful competitor for the VANs. In Scandinavia, the relatively low cost of suitable lines also makes them the first choice for EDI users; indeed, they question why anyone would need a VAN. Scandinavians also prefer packet switching for JIT deliveries, contending that there must be some delay with a VAN. In fact, both INS and AT&T Istel deny this, pointing out that unless translation is required, which it would not be for such traffic, the message is deposited in the mailbox immediately it is sent. The fact that Rover Group is a successful user of JIT deliveries by a network supports this view.

In any case, some of the existing trading communities in Scandinavia are closed, with a number of vendors supplying the vehicle makers only—Saab and Volvo. There are no time zone problems, working hours are common, and owing to the relatively low volume of manufacture, the traffic is not heavy.

Some doubts are cast on the security of packet switching used for PDNs, but the principle of operation ensures security. When a message is taken from storage, it is divided into small packets of data and fed into a multiplexer. Packets from several messages are sent by the multiplexer sequentially in random order, and then demultiplexed back into individual messages at the other end.

Therefore, it is almost impossible for the message to be intercepted and decoded. There are also passwords and signing-on procedures, while closed user groups, inaccessible to others, can be established.

The costs definitely favour the public data network, with a throughput of 5Mbytes/week costing £80 at 2.4kbit/s, against £300 over an INS leased line of 9.6kbit/s.

One of the bigger operators of a PDN is Transpac, the subsidiary of France Telecom. In practice, it controls the French EDI market, largely because a licence is required by any other company than wishes to operate a leased line, and the VANs business is very tightly regulated. Transpac is involved in the national clearing system for banks, and has established an organisation with Groupe Bull to handle EDI communications between French local authorities and government ministries. However, bureaucracy is holding up the development of this potentially huge network.

French VAN enters the UK

Transpac has now entered the British market with the purchase of the data network operated formerly by London Regional Transport. It will offer a connection to its packet switching network in France in 1992, plans a total coverage of the UK by 1993, and eventually a network over the whole of Europe. Although this development, and others that will follow, would appear to limit the need for VANs, the existing providers of VANs expect their specialist knowledge and services to yield a market.

Future for VANs

There are several reasons for this optimism. First, the true costs of operating over a PDN are not merely the line costs, whereas the VAN charges (See Chapter Thirteen) are inclusive. Included in the VAN charges are security, a wide range of functions, and auditing. In addition, a VAN may be accessed by any user, with any type or make of computer from a PC upward operating any software, with any message format, and any recognised protocols. Were a large user with 200 trading partners to adopt the point-to-point approach through a PDN, it would incur considerable costs in managing the system.

To summarise, a VAN is the obvious choice in the UK at present, but in Europe, the PDN is the main service used. In the future, the Continental approach will spread, but despite the emergence of standards, such as X.400 discussed in the next chapter, the VANs will remain attractive to many users.

Chapter Seven

Message formats and protocols established

Choice of proven standards

Move to Edifact messages—in time

X.400 the protocol of the future

MANY discussions and conferences about EDI seem to be dominated by concerns about standards—why there is more than one, which one to use, and the future pattern. This is not a subject that need concern senior managers, despite the apparent controversy—indeed, the best thing they can do is to ignore all the abbreviations, acronyms and names for the different messages, and remember EDI only.

A good parallel between EDI standards is that with television standards worldwide: almost all users in the USA and Japan are oblivious to the fact that they cannot use their televisions or their video tapes in Europe, and it is only in special cases that a person finds the different standards actually impinges on his life.

Proven message formats

Actually, the situation in EDI is rather better, in that translation software is in use where it is needed, so a message in one format can be translated into another format. Nevertheless, there are different standards and protocols. These were developed by groups of users or bodies set up by users, and one reason for Britain's leadership in Europe in the use of EDI is that bodies such as The Simpler Trade Procedures Board (SITPRO) and The Article Numbering Association (ANA) helped the establishment of standard message formats that met users' needs.

The standards governing EDI messages are:

☐ Message formats: These govern the type of information that may or must be transmitted, in what sequence that data must be transmitted, the nature of the data to be transmitted, such as the length of a data item, and the type of characters used;

☐ Syntax: This defines the character set in use; special codes that separate different items to give the message a format; the header and trailer, or envelope which identifies the beginning and end of the message;

☐ File transfer protocol: This governs the telecommunications protocols.

For example, Odette has a common message format, but the syntax may be either UN-GTDI or Edifact. There is also a standard file transfer protocol.

EDI was used first in the USA, where a standard was developed by ANSI. Other bodies have established standards, as mentioned earlier. The main message formats in use are:

☐ ANSI X12: used in the USA and Canada;
☐ Tradacoms: in UK and Europe;
☐ Odette: UN-GTDI used mainly by the European motor industry;
☐ UN/Edifact: The international standard developed under the auspices of the UN.

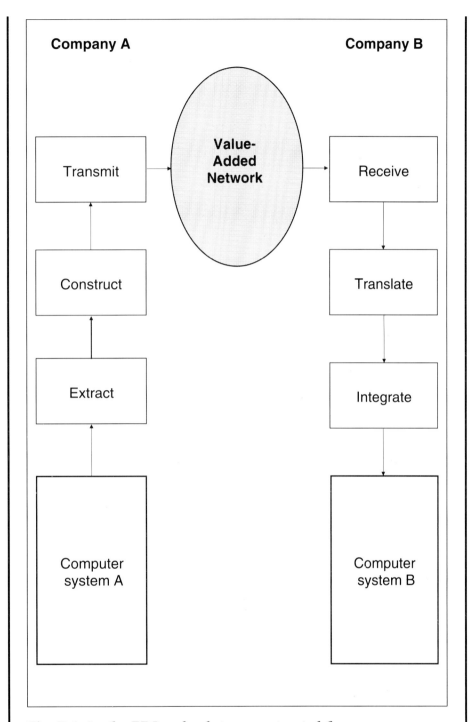

Fig. 7.1. In the EDI cycle, data are extracted from an applications file, a message is constructed in a suitable format and transmitted to the network; it is accessed by the trading partner which translates—or deformats—the message and passes it into the relevant applications software

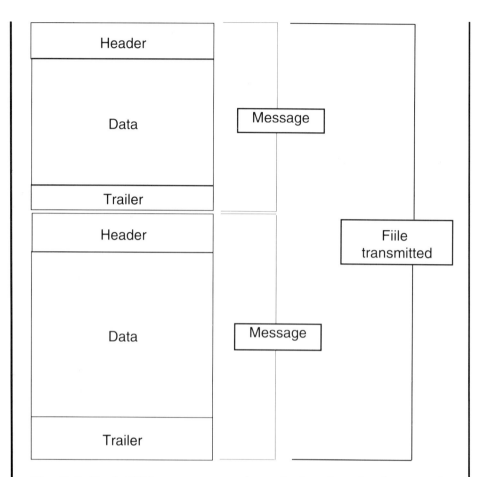

Fig. 7.2. Each EDI message consists of a header, the data, and a trailer; several messages can be included in one file

Move to Edifact

Already, moves are afoot to reduce the number of standards in use. For example, German car manufacturers use a VDA standard, but the VDA has agreed that all future messages will follow the Odette syntax. In Sweden, 200 suppliers to Saab and Volvo are already using Edifact syntax with Odette messages, while users of Odette in France, Spain and Italy are also using Edifact. The next versions of Odette messages, to be released in 1994, will be Edifact messages.

In the USA, Europe and Japan, it has been agreed that Edifact should be used wherever practical, and that groups should migrate from their own standards to Edifact. The aim is that by 1995, there will be a combination of Edifact messages and X.400 protocols.

Inertia of old standards

In practice, existing messages are likely to remain in use for many years. Users that have gone to the expense of developing special messages to suit either Odette or Tradacoms are not keen to develop new messages in Edifact soon afterwards. For example, Ford uses VDA standards and it has no intention of changing to Odette, while Rover Group is not keen to change its special messages to Edifact. The reasons are simple enough; Ford could change its messages without too much difficulty, but its vendors spread across Europe might take a very long time to switch, burdening Ford with the need to operate two sets of messages for at least six months. Even so, all users such as Ford recognise the need for standardisation, and should take it into account when new messages are created.

Another reason for the delay in switching to Edifact is that few Edifact messages have reached the stage where they can be used reliably, whereas larger sets of messages are available in other formats. This is inevitable when an international body develops standards which must be approved by all parties before being accepted. By the end of 1991, it was expected that 14 trade or materials management messages would have reached stage 1 or 2—the level at which they can be used reliably. However, the accent has been on documents suitable for international trade, such as those required by Customs, so Edifact is still far from being the first choice.

Any potential user of EDI wants to be sure that there are enough messages available to adopt EDI without the need to keep changing messages. However, since it will take six to 12 months for most new users to be up and running, and then they will require one or two messages only to start with, the absence of a full suite of messages need not hold back the implementation of EDI—so long as they are being developed.

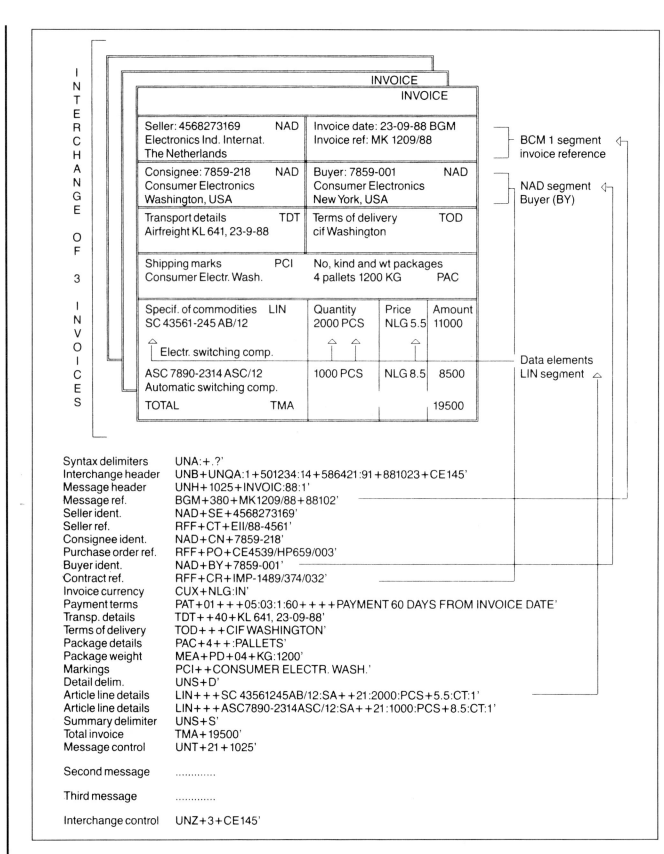

Fig. 7.3. A paper invoice, top, compared with the same information sent by EDI, below it

Wide range of Odette messages

Even so, availability of messages is important, and the large number of messages available is one reason why Odette and Tradacoms are used widely. Currently, there are 26 Odette messages, some of which are approved for use in the UK only. Messages are revised every two years, so Version 3 messages have been in use for at least four years, and have been modified twice to take account of users suggestions and complaints. Version 3 messages are available for:

- ☐ INVOIC—invoice;
- ☐ INVLTR—invoice trailer;
- ☐ AVIEXP—Despatch advice;
- ☐ DELINS—Delivery instruction.

There are 15 Version 2 messages including:

- ☐ ENQUIRY—Enquiry;
- ☐ OFFERR—response to enquiry with a price and conditions;
- ☐ ORDERR—Order, either blanket or stand-alone;
- ☐ KANBAN—Kanban signal authorising vendor to ship goods;
- ☐ REPDEL—Reply to delivery instruction;
- ☐ SYNCRO—Request for synchronised delivery;
- ☐ FORDIS—Forecast of despatch;
- ☐ REMADV—Remittance advice.

These messages are geared toward the relationship between vendor and customer in manufacturing industry. For example, there are eight messages to cover the ordering phase, five for the delivery instruction phase, three for the goods despatch, and seven for financial settlement. Among the specialised messages is INVTLR which is required to summarise VAT details for H.M. Customs & Excise in the UK.

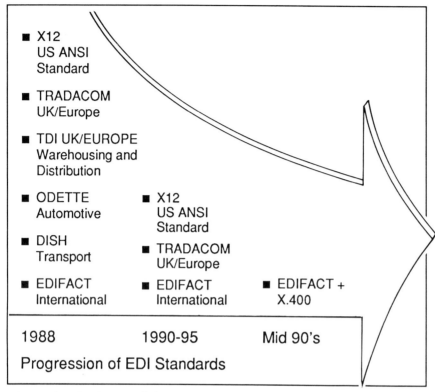

■ X12
US ANSI
Standard

■ TRADACOM
UK/Europe

■ TDI UK/EUROPE
Warehousing and
Distribution

■ ODETTE   ■ X12
Automotive   US ANSI
                    Standard
■ DISH
Transport   ■ TRADACOM
                    UK/Europe

■ EDIFACT   ■ EDIFACT   ■ EDIFACT +
International   International   X.400

1988   1990-95   Mid 90's

Progression of EDI Standards

Fig. 7.4. The hope of the various organisations promoting EDI is that Edifact and X.400 will become the universal standards by 1995-6

There are 18 fully-proven Tradacoms messages; another seven are available, but will not be published formally by the Article Numbering Association (ANA) which controls development, until 1992. Included in the messages are:

☐ Price information;
☐ Product information;
☐ Availability report;
☐ Order;
☐ Delivery notification;
☐ Delivery confirmation;
☐ Acknowledgement of order;
☐ Stock adjustment
☐ Credit note;
☐ Invoice.

Although UN/Edifact messages are lagging the others, the situation is improving. Following the meeting of the UN Working Party in September 1991, 18 messages are now approved at Status 2. These include:

- ☐ Credit advice;
- ☐ Customs cargo message;
- ☐ Customs declaration;
- ☐ Customs response;
- ☐ Invoice;
- ☐ Purchase order;
- ☐ Remittance advice;
- ☐ Payment order.

Although these are biased toward international trading, another 15 messages, including Just-in-Time delivery, Delivery schedule message, Despatch advice and Quotation are at Status 1. Another 22 messages are at Status 0. Therefore, Edifact messages are available for many transactions, and a full range of Edifact messages should be fully proven by 1992-3. The wide range of Odette messages is one reason why it is being used so widely, however.

X.400 the standard of the future

When it comes to the manner in which the messages are transmitted, a set of protocols is needed to control transmission of data, and to allow the data to be received correctly by the other computer. There is a number of internationally agreed protocols for the transmission of data, and the important ones for EDI are X.25, which is used for PDNs, and X.400. Both are standards for file transfer protocols developed by the CCITT, the international telecommunications body. X.25 is used widely for EDI in Scandinavia, by some users in France and in Belgium. For use over the X.25 network, the Odette File Transfer Profile (OFTP), which allows multiple addressing, is becoming a de facto standard in many areas, and is likely to remain in use for many years.

In due course, X.400 will be used, owing to its flexibility. It is a universal standard to cover all types of electronic message, including electronic mail with different outputs—fax, telex and EDI.

As mentioned earlier, these standards are quite independent of those that define the format of the EDI message itself, but there was a problem in that EDI and X.400 overlapped in areas such as the details of the recipient and sender. In March 1988, therefore, a group was established to resolve these differences. Meanwhile, some VANs and large users adopted an interim set of rules to cover the overlap, and these are in use by Cefic, the chemical industry's pan-European EDI initiative. The results of the review—the 1988 version of X.400—are now available.

An X.400 message consists of an envelope and contents—or a header and body. The advantage of this approach is that the actual message can be long or short, and can consist of any type of data, including text, binary files, such as the data from a spreadsheet, or Computer Aided Design (CAD) data.

Excellent procedures for the tracing of message movement are available, and the messages may be encrypted. There is a common addressing format, and X.400 messages can, in theory, be sent almost anywhere in the world.

Edifice, the group representing electronics companies, is pressing for a European standard to be developed for identifying users of message handling systems. It recommends that a single unique name be registered for each user, so that trading partners can continue to use the same identification, irrespective of the message handling system it employs. Such a scheme is essential, in the same way that each user has a unique fax number.

International network for X.400

X.400 is becoming available rapidly. For EDI transmissions, a receiving address is required, and the X.435 standard—previously PEDI—covers this. Therefore, the standard has moved far enough for it to be implemented internationally. It has been agreed recently that the X.400 services, operated by Transpac in France, the Deutsche Bundespost Telekom, Teleo in Italy, PTT Telecom (Netherlands), TS1 Telefonica Servicios (Spain), Sevate (Portugal), RTT Belgium, Televerket (Sweden),

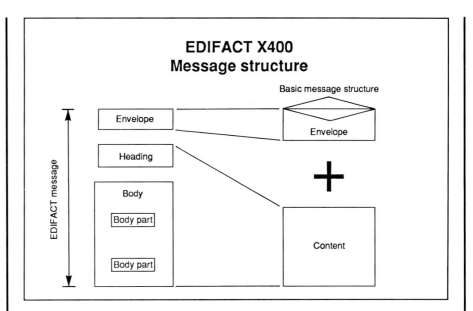

Fig. 7.5. X.400 can handle messages of many different types, including CAD data

Radio Austria and the Swiss PTT, will be interconnected by the end of 1991, so before long corporations will be able to interconnect to others in most of Europe.

AT&T Istel has launched an X.400 service, while INS has started trials on an X.400 gateway into Tradanet; the service should be available by the end of 1991. However, INS expects demand to be limited for some time—both the software and the network service for X.400 are costly, while many teething troubles have been encountered by those setting up networks for themselves. At present X.400 is suitable only for large multinational corporations, and the pioneering users tend to be computer companies, such as Digital Equipment and Hewlett Packard. Other users include BP Oil and ICI, while the British government's GOSIP project for data transmission between government departments includes X.400.

One set of standards for all?

By the mid-1990s, the hope is that industry worldwide will be using X.400 and Edifact, and there is some controversy as to whether most will channel their X.400 traffic through VANs or not; needless to say, the VANs are optimistic they will receive most of the business. In any case, it is likely that other message formats and protocols will remain in use beyond that date, and that not all Edifact messages will be compatible. Since each trading community is limited in size, that apparent conflict is unlikely to limit the use of EDI. However, the larger trading communities become, the more care will be needed in ascertaining that all newcomers are actually interpreting the syntax and protocols in the same way.

Worldwide EDI for all manufacturers

For many years, the EDI community has been attempting to nurture standards while allowing use to grow sufficiently to make standardisation worthwhile. There is a well-established organisation promoting Edifact and the merging of standards, so the way to universal standards is open. As long as users and these bodies continue to move toward the goals of standardisation, truly international EDI, combining the network of the telephone service with an internationally understood language, will be available.

A purchaser in Birmingham—England or the USA—will be able to look up a potential vendor in Bombay or Nagasaki in the trade directory in his database, find the EDI mailbox number, and fire off a request for a quotation—all in a message of universal standard. Since the recipient will know immediately what each data element refers to, he will be able to translate the facts of the enquiry from English into his own language much more easily than if he had received a letter, and reply to the inquiry more easily as well. Moreover, once a contract is agreed, the Customs, freight forwarder and shipping companies will all be able to carry out their part of the transaction speedily and efficiently with the minimum of misunderstanding. Truly international business will be a reality, thanks to EDI.

Chapter Eight

Any computer, available software

From a PC and modem upward

Translation and other packages off the shelf

EDI gateway the best long-term approach

TO START trading electronically, 'all' that is required is a personal computer (PC), a modem, printer and a software package, at a total cost of £2,000-£4,000. Although the cost of entry is such that even a small supplier can hardly claim not to be able to afford to use EDI, it can snare managers into the delusion that implementation is trivial and does not require much of their attention—an error that will result in the company failing to gain the true benefits of EDI.

Since the whole point of EDI is that it enables functions to be automated, connections are needed between the EDI system and other in-house applications. Printing out documents from the PC which receives the messages is not EDI. Therefore, the cost of equipment is only the beginning, but it is also the beginning of the savings—too often managers equate the initial cost with the savings made in the first few months and complain that the new system is a failure. In reality, the savings will increase with time, and need to be justified over a three- to five-year span—well beyond the imagination of short-termists.

Setting up EDI requires considerable management effort at both strategic and operational levels, as will be discussed in Chapter Thirteen. First, however, a basic understanding of the type of hardware and software is required.

Most manufacturing companies, even if they are small specialists, will now be using at least a PC for some of their administrative functions, such as accounts and VAT returns. The implementation of EDI will give them the opportunity of expanding computerisation. Larger companies using minicomputers or mainframes can add EDI software and arrange their machines to handle the extra application through a terminal. Alternatively, they can dedicate a PC to EDI, and connect it to their computer system, an approach often adopted when a company is uncertain about the extent of EDI transactions. It has the advantage that during the learning stage, the machine can be independent of the main computer system.

Plenty of power and memory for the PC

Although one of the cheapest IBM-compatible PCs will handle EDI, most users consider an AT compatible—one built around an Intel 80286 processor—the minimum practical machine. In any case, the prices of the more powerful 386 and 486 machines are falling quite sharply, and in some cases cost no more than an AT compatible. Since 386 or 486 machines are able to operate some functions in the background, and are usually equipped with greater memory than an AT compatible, they are more useful for extensive EDI operations. In any event, the long-term view should be taken when investing in EDI hardware and the more powerful machine bought. Also, the machine should be part of a family that can be upgraded with the addition of a server, and that can be integrated into a network of PCs.

There is a general trend to increased processing power in PCs which have far lower overall costs/transaction than minicomputers or mainframes. In the next few years, RISC (reduced instruction set computer) processors will come into use for the most expensive PCs, further boosting processing power. Similar improvements will be made in minicomputers, so the trend is toward more distributed processing, and less use of mainframes. This trend also needs to be taken into account when purchasing hardware for EDI. For example, Advance Tapes (International), a company with 280 employees and a turnover of £20 million, decided four years ago that its mainframe was not cost-effective and replaced it with a network of 50 PCs, the most powerful of which are Apricot 486 machines. The change has reduced all costs significantly and has proved most effective.

Apart from a computer, the other main requirements are a printer and a modem which converts digital signals to and from the analogue signals used in telephony. Nor should the modem be a bargain-basement model; if it is, it will almost certainly be unable to perform some functions that are required. For example, high-speed error correction, in which the data are checked continuously for errors, is essential. With this software built-in, when an error is detected, the data are resent.

Normally, modems capable of transmitting at 1,200 bit/second or 2,400 bit/s are used on the telephone network, but 9,600 bit/s is practical, and is preferable. A modem capable of transmitting at 2,400 bit/s is the minimum for anything but occasional EDI.

However, once the ISDN network becomes widespread, telephone signals will all be digital, so modems will be redundant. ISDN is not likely to be in widespread use in the UK before 1995-6—not least because BT is not marketing it aggressively—so a modem bought in 1992 should remain in service for at least three years and perhaps five or six years.

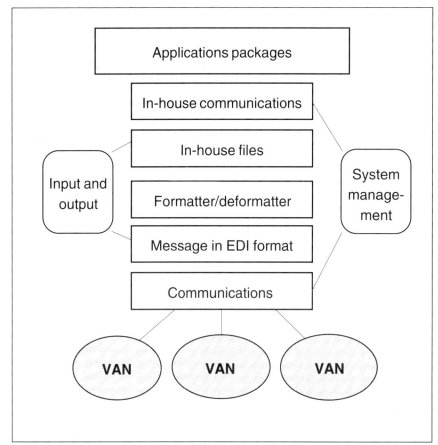

Fig. 8.1. Software is required for several functions, for system management and also for inputting and outputting of data

Choosing software

In parallel with the decision on hardware, the user must choose some software. This is an equally critical decision, particularly since some of the software packages for PCs are subsets of those for mainframes or minicomputers lacking some useful features. Therefore, careful investigation and selection is important.

But what actually must EDI software do? Basically, EDI software consists of:

☐ Communications functions, to control the rate of transfer of data and send them with the necessary protocols and so on;

☐ Translation, to and from the format required for the partner—for example, Edifact, Odette or Tradacoms;

☐ Status report function.

Also required are the abilities to trace a document through all the stages of its journey, and to update files that are in use. Most users will also want to be able to send messages to several different trading partners in one batch—not all software can do this. In some cases, all modules are integrated into one package, and in others separate modules are supplied.

Although those are basic requirements, the user needs to consider his likely use, and will almost certainly require the ability to:

☐ Use different message formats to trade with different partners;
☐ Trade over different networks;
☐ Transmit a number of different documents, in some cases with different versions of one document;
☐ Archive documents, which will become essential business records—indicating the tax point for VAT, for example;
☐ Route data into existing applications software.

Before the actual software package is considered, the user needs to decide on the conceptual approach to handling EDI messages. This is most important because companies usually start with one or two messages only—the receipt of orders and the transmission of invoices, for example—and so there is a tendency to handle EDI in the department involved first. With that approach the problems will multiply as EDI develops.

When an extra message is adopted, another department and another applications package are likely to be involved. The people in that department may need different functions, with the result that much time can be spent by the IT staff writing programs or altering the way the EDI messages are routed. Each time a new department is involved, there is potential for conflict and complication. Clearly, this is not a sound approach, except in small companies where there is just one department handling all administration.

In addition, when the system is configured, multiple
networks need to be taken into account; in some cases,
where this was not done, the company ended up buying
a second PC and software to trade with a partner on a
different network.

Gateway concept

For these reasons, many EDI users have now adopted the
EDI gateway concept in which one machine—either real
or logical—is dedicated to handling the EDI messages. It
sits as a gateway between the networks and/or leased
lines and the various departments in the company. The
functions of the gateway are to:

☐   Receive the file from a partner and translate it from
       the EDI format, called the network interface form, to
       a neutral file, often called an applications interface;
☐   Transmit the neutral file to the applications software
       in the relevant department;
☐   Perform functions in reverse sequence to files sent by
       each department to the gateway.

In this way, the technical requirements of EDI are kept
quite separate from the business applications software.
The programmer responsible for the gateway will be
concerned purely with its successful operation, and will
be able to ensure that the company can trade with
multiple partners over multiple networks—as and when
needed. At the same time, the applications software need
not be affected directly by the use of EDI, although some
changes may be needed. For example, it may be necessary
to modify the software that handles orders to identify the
customer by a code. Also, some extra modules, to control
transmissions of a batch of acknowledgements of
purchase orders to the gateway, instead of one by one,
may be needed.

Overall, the gateway approach gives maximum flexibility
while the cost of implementation is reduced. Several large
companies have adopted the gateway approach,
including Digital Equipment, Lucas Industries and Texas
Instruments. Lucas Industries has operated a gateway on
its IBM 370/390 mainframe since 1987, and routes

messages from the UK to customers in Britain, other European countries and North America. Over 75,000 messages are handled monthly—an average of 100/hour over seven days a week, 24 hours a day.

Software to handle all documents

A vendor supplying a major manufacturer handles a considerable number of documents related to the products involved. There are purchase orders, to be followed by call-off orders, perhaps according to a JIT schedule. Internal orders are raised, the stock of raw materials interrogated and, where appropriate, orders are placed on suppliers. Then, manufacturing needs to

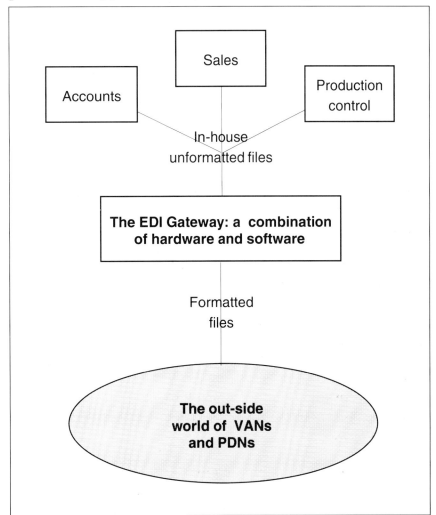

Fig. 8.2. The use of an EDI gateway keeps EDI separate from applications software, and facilitates a strategic approach

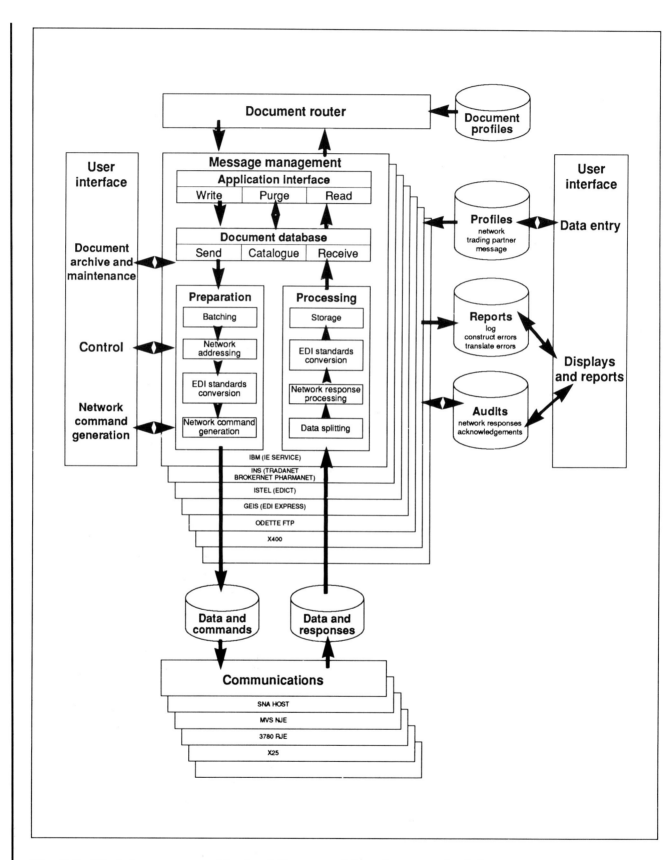

Fig. 8.3. SD-Scicon can provide the full range of functions required for multple-network, multiple-message formats on a variety of computers

confirm it can meet the schedule, the order is acknowledged, and in due course an advance notice of delivery is sent, while there is the advice note itself, and finally an invoice.

When the EDI system and its software are selected, all these documents need to be considered—and whether such documents will be needed for electronic trading. For example, invoices should not be needed with EDI. Since several major manufacturers operate self-billing schemes, most potential users will be able to find a trading partner with some experience of the way these operate.

Small manufacturers may doubt that they require or can afford a gateway. However, since a gateway requires no more than a PC and the relevant software, the concept can be adopted by a small manufacturer. In the same way that a mainframe can be used as a gateway, so a PC can be used as a gateway part-time when the volume of transmissions is small. PCs can be set up also to operate some functions in the background automatically, so that the operator need not be aware that the PC has logged onto the network and downloaded a message—one of the more powerful PCs is preferable for this work.

Understandable data elements

Although the functions of EDI software must match the requirements of the user, the way in which the data are inputted is also important. Some software is written such that the input data follows the structure and terminology of the EDI message itself; this requires that the user has some understanding of the way in which the messages are constructed. This is clearly unsuitable for most users.

Instead, a package in which there is a functional input screen, with the description of data elements being understood easily by all operators, is needed. In the ideal situation, the user should be able to write a front-end by following simple instructions so that the descriptions can be tailored or changed to suit terms used by the company, but many will find this is unnecessary.

Although EDI software is being improved all the time, there are still many problems in its full implementation. For example, one weakness is that standard applications software packages used by industry lack the modules needed to suit EDI. Spreadsheets and accounts packages should include some relevant functions, such as the ability to export data in the desired form to a gateway. This is not a question of formatting the data for EDI, but of allowing the data to be transmitted in the sequence required by the EDI software.

Custom or off-the-shelf?

Although some companies may be tempted to write all their own software, it is not realistic to write the translation packages. Complete packages are also available, but if companies wish to have their own software, a good approach is to purchase standard packages and link them together with custom-developed modules. Measures to provide necessary levels of security can also be produced in-house.

Of the standard translation packages, SD-Scicon's Interbridge, developed to format and deformat Edifact and Tradacoms messages, is typical. The copyright is held by the Board for the Simplification of International Trade Procedures (SITPRO). Interbridge is written in ANSI COBOL, and there is just one version of source code, with separate modules of machine-dependent code. It can be used on mainframes, minicomputers and PCs.

When using Interbridge, the operator is presented with a number of tables which are set up to suit the application. Amendments are made to the tables only, and not to the basic program. The price of Interbridge Release 4 varies from £1,225 for a PC to £3,000 for a mainframe. Another program, Intercept-Plus, is recommended and marketed by INS for PCs. The presentation to the user is by menus, and it incorporates the functions required by most users. For example, it supports Edifact, Tradacoms and Odette, is suitable for connections to all networks, and is designed for unattended operation, with up to 42 sessions a week. AT&T Istel's Edict PC is a similar product.

Among the suppliers of software that have specialised in the Odette message standard is Data Interchange, formerly part of Perkins Engines. It has three main

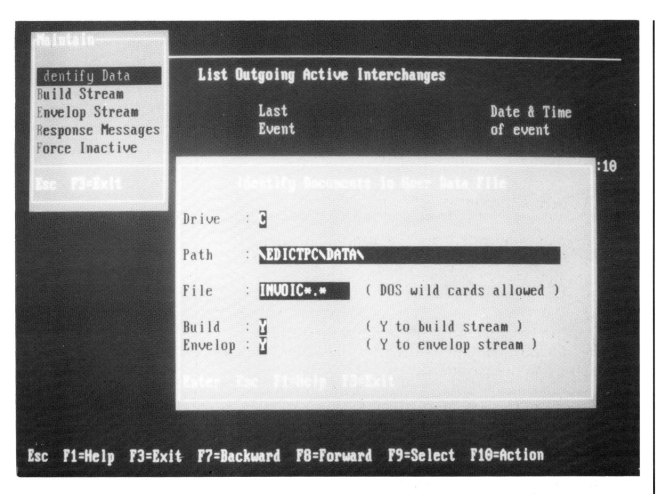

Fig. 8.4 . The face of EDI: one of the screens the user sees with AT&T Istel's Edict-PC, an inexpensive software package

packages: Odex for communications; Xlate for translation, and Direx for document data entry and reporting. The Odex file transfer program, which handles communications can:

☐ Transmit and receive Odette files directly to a trading partner or through a VAN;
☐ Handle EDI and unstructured files;
☐ Produce reports on the files in process or already processed;
☐ Recover fully from a breakdown;
☐ Support Edifact;
☐ Call out and receive messages automatically;
☐ Carry out a comprehensive audit trail;
☐ Split and merge EDI files;
☐ Handle data compressed for faster throughput.

Compower, a subsidiary of British Coal, developed its Supplyline software to suit manufacturing industry as well. Initially, British Coal wanted a package to use with AT&T Istel's AT&T EDI and which it could sell cheaply to smaller vendors. The package has since been taken up by a number of hubs of EDI networks, including British Rail and Black and Decker. Also intended for small users is Edistart, which is marketed by BT.

Each of the network operators also supplies approved software for its VAN, while there are a number of other specialists in the EDI software business, such as Compument Software, Gentran, Pensus, and Ibix Computing which designed its Blue Rainbow software specially for IBM AS/400 mainframe computers, although there is now a PC version. In North America, Supply Tech claims that its STX12 package is the most popular EDI software with Boeing, Caterpillar, General Motors and IBM being among its customers.

These and other companies are able to provide suitable software, but before the choice is made the user needs to decide how EDI is to be used, and to compare the software with the specific requirements. In existing software packages, audit trails tend to be less comprehensive than might be desired, while manuals are rarely ideal. However, most attention should be paid to how the EDI package can connect to the in-house applications packages, since this can be a weak link; success is vital if EDI is to be integrated sufficiently to give the desired benefits.

When selecting hardware and software, the long-term view needs to be taken. Eventually, a new user will need a combination of hardware and software to:

☐ Send messages to, and receive messages from multiple VANs and over the PDN with differing protocols;
☐ Send and receive messages in multiple message formats;
☐ Call up the VAN automatically to look for messages;
☐ Audit message routes;
☐ Obtain the status of its messages;
☐ Route messages to applications software automatically;
☐ Maintain security of access to its EDI gateway.

These requirements need to be considered from the start, and incorporated into any IT strategy the company may have. In some companies, the use of EDI may be the first attempt at communicating data between computers, in which case it should become the watershed leading to automated administration.

Chapter Nine

Bar codes for lean materials handling

Comprehensive coding, agreed internationally

Automates goods receiving

Controls routing and stock levels

DESPITE the success achieved by big retail chains with the use of bar codes, British manufacturers have been slow to adopt them. This is surprising, not only because the delivery chain to a superstore is similar to that to a factory, but also because many Japanese manufacturers use them to route components automatically into their plants. As mentioned earlier, the supply chain of retail stores and assembly plants are virtually common until the final stage, so there is every reason for manufacturers to use bar codes.

In any case, evidence indicates that the use of bar codes produces worthwhile savings. According to a survey by Kurt Salmon Associates and Andersen Consulting in the USA, an investment of $1 in bar coding brings a return of $2.20 to a manufacturer. Their use allows aspects of the supply chain to be automated, and is a key to a reduction in indirect labour, which becomes a proportionally greater burden as the level of automation in manufacture increases. Of course, a substantial reduction in non-productive labour is part of any move toward lean manufacture.

International standards

Like EDI, bar codes are based on standards, but in this case, the international standard has been accepted widely. They are administered by the EAN, the International Article Numbering Association, and in the UK by the Article Numbering Association (ANA). ANA allocates bar codes to members, which must pay a small annual subscription and a fee for the allocation of numbers. Incidentally, EAN is developing a series of Edifact messages for international use called Eancom.

Within the EAN bar coding system, each identification number consists of 13 digits represented by bars, of which the first seven digits identify the company. The following five digits identify the product—the permutations allow 100,000 items to be coded—and there is one digit to act as a check on the code. There are also 13 digits for the despatch unit or product number and 'logistical variant', while there are supplementary codes for batch numbers and production data.

In practice, therefore, bar codes can be used for all relevant data on an advice note relating to the components, the batch size and number, and the supplier's reference. A bar code called Party Information contains the address and contact person for each physical

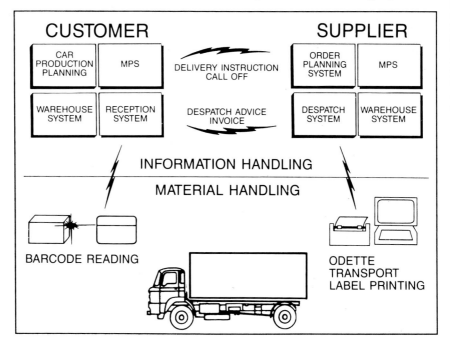

Fig. 9.1. Bar codes complete the supplier-manufacturer loop

and financial location. Therefore, all the information required can be included in bar codes.

Popular in Sweden

Although the Odette group has taken up bar coding for automatic identification, it is the Swedish manufacturers that perhaps use them most. As mentioned in Chapter Four, Rover Group and Ford are moving more slowly toward their general use. Pilot projects are under way, however, and in Britain, Ford, Rover Group, Peugeot Talbot and Nissan are now requesting that the Odette bar codes be used by a small number of suppliers.

In Sweden many vendors adopted bar codes before EDI. Therefore, although only 200 vendors use EDI, 300 are using the Odette bar coded label, including 70% of Volvo's suppliers. In France, 80% of shipments to vehicle manufacturers are said to be bar coded, while Citroen, Ford, ENASA, Nissan and SEAT are all introducing bar codes in Spain; approximately 200 vendors there are involved in the programme.

The latest version of the Odette bar coded transport label is version 1 revision 3.1. It is printed on a standard A5 label and is based on the alphanumeric Code 39 symbols. Since this would be too big for some pallets used in the electronics industry and for some components in the motor industry, there is also a label for small packages, and one for steel bars. The standard label consists of:

☐ The part name of the recipient;
☐ Despatch advice note number;
☐ Weight;
☐ Supplier's name;
☐ Part number;
☐ Quantity;
☐ Supplier's identification number;
☐ Label serial number.

A separate advice note is not needed, since the bar codes can be scanned—a light pen, fixed or hand-held, or a fixed CCD scanner can be used—and the data captured automatically to the computer system in goods receiving. Ideally, to automate the process, the pallet should pass a fixed scanner, but owing to the different sizes of pallets in use this is not always practical.

Such a system demands trust between vendor and customer, and this trust comes more easily with the close relationship obtained by electronic trading. It is not likely to develop through the use of bar coded pallets alone, simply because the time required to process the data, combined with the inevitable errors, would not give the customer sufficient confidence in the data to allow its relationship with vendor to grow.

Bar codes fit with EDI

Bar codes fit well with EDI because the data on the call-off order serve as the basis for the delivery advice note—the supplier merely adds extra information, such as the batch number, to that provided by the customer. Therefore, the same data can be interpreted and printed out to form the label. Initially, customers will want one of their employees to check visually that the pallet is full. However, with JIT deliveries the returnable pallets are purpose-built to suit the component so the storemen can see at a glance whether they are full or not. Once EDI is in operation, the customer receives advice notes in his computer system at the same time the goods arrive, so confidence that the ordered goods are actually being delivered is high. The customer can also use the bar code label to provide the information to route the pallets automatically to the line.

For example, although Oki Electric, the Japanese electronics company, does not use EDI, bar coded labels are attached to all pallets sent to the factory where it produces small printers. Each pallet carries a bar code which is read automatically when it arrives, and the data are entered first into the computer controlling the automatic storage/retrieval warehouse to allocate a rack. When the pallet is required at the assembly line, the bar

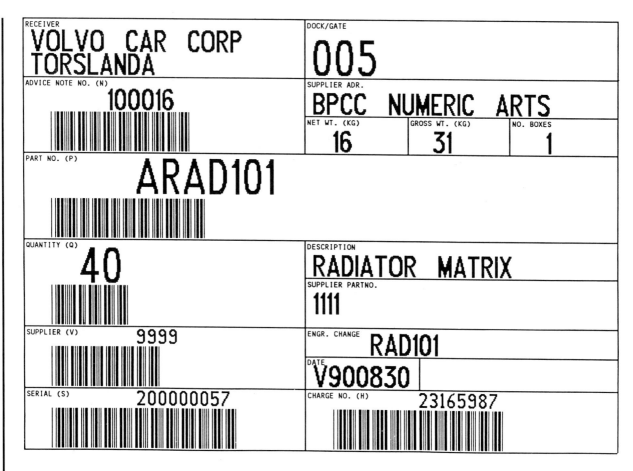

Fig. 9.2. Whereas with conventional progress-chasing several different telephone calls are required, each prone to error, with EDI one set of data is sent once

code is used to identify which pallet should be withdrawn. The pallet is transferred to an automated guided vehicle, and the data input from the bar code are used to identify the station to which the pallet should be taken. Components are picked directly from the pallets at the line, either by operator or by robot.

Bar code routes pallet to assembly line

For integration of bar codes into the EDI system, further processes are involved. For example, after the bar code on the pallet has been scanned, the data need to be fed into the computer. The data can then be reconciled automatically with the advice note received from the vendor. In addition, the entry of the scanned label into the computer could be used to indicate the time when the goods are considered to have been bought and to indicate routing to the assembly line.

When the pallet in use at the assembly line becomes empty and is returned to the stores, the same label could be scanned to indicate that another pallet was required—a method of operating the desired pull-type system to minimise stock.

Replenishment of pallets at the line

In some cases, to suit JIT, the vendor delivers directly to the side of the line, replacing empty pallets or containers with full ones. In that case, the trigger for a delivery could be made by the operator scanning the bar code with a light pen when one full pallet only remains. In this case, the action of the operator would normally result in a call-off order being placed with the vendor automatically. Clearly, the purchasing officer does not need to intervene in such a transaction; Japanese manufacturers have allowed automatic operation of such deliveries for many years.

Several companies have introduced bar codes before adopting EDI, such as Rowntree Mackintosh which was able to simplify control of the 2,000 different packages it generates each year. Bar codes are used both for its products, and for the materials from vendors. Initially, the use of bar codes eliminated the need for data to be keyed in—the minimum benefit they offer.

Although several manufacturers use bar codes without EDI, the real benefits come when the two are used together. Once EDI is being used as well, there is no need to print a paper advice note. Identification is faster and more efficient, while the continuous monitoring of the quantities of components delivered simplifies stock control. Another benefit of bar codes, which applies equally to EDI, is that since the contents and location of the data fields are standard, there is no need to translate into a foreign language when components are exported.

EDI goes a long way toward automating the supply chain, and bar codes can close the loop, eliminating errors and reducing administrative costs.

Chapter Ten

Cutting the cost of administration

Operational costs cut 25-60%

Integrated EDI automates transactions

Stock levels reduced

THERE are two ways to use EDI: as a strategic weapon or as an operational tool. In adopting EDI, some companies look immediately to new ways of doing business; more conservative managers expect merely to cut the cost of operations. However, all managers should expect to improve operating efficiency and make some strategic gains.

Whatever the long-term aim, the operational side needs to be considered first. For example, to alter the relationship with vendors the first requirement is to change the form of the business documents. The transfer of an existing document from paper to an electronic equivalent is certain to be inefficient, not least because the electronic format imposes disciplines not apparent with paper, while the contents of paper documents have expanded over time, often without redundant items being eliminated.

Therefore, whatever ambitions a manufacturer has with EDI, a review of paperwork comes before an attempt is made to change strategy. (The approach to starting EDI is discussed in the next chapter). Moreover, the way in which a company operates its accounts, orders and delivery systems influences its approach.

True automation at last

Where will the savings come, and how can they be quantified? The savings will come from the use of true automation in the office. Many offices are now equipped with either many terminals or PCs, but few are automated. Most resemble a factory in which rows of automatic machines have been installed without any inter-connecting automation. It is as if there were an operator at each machine in the plant, loading and unloading the components being turned out by the machine faster than he could handle them. He also has to hand them to someone else for transfer to the next machine. The overall output is slightly higher than that of the previous plant, but the cost of the automatic machines is far greater than of the old machines that were operated manually. However, with some extra investment in automatic handling and gauging equipment, the output will rise and the 100 men can be replaced by 10-20.

EDI and associated electronic transfers offer the same long-term benefits in automating the office. But just as it took time and overseas competition for manufacturers to gain the full potential with factory automation, so time is needed with EDI.

In the office, the reasons for the lack of true automation are many: much software was written on the premise that one person would use it, and automation of commands is primitive and unreliable, especially when used on networks. When computers were introduced, they replaced typewriters, and the ex-typists tend to operate them as typewriters. In any case, software allowing full integration of all functions is not widely available. Meanwhile, management and office staff alike are suspicious of the automation of jobs they consider need brainwork.

EDI changes all this because the method of operation must be reviewed and forms need to be redesigned for its implementation. This forces managers to look further into operating techniques, and enables them to automate office activities.

Administration automated

By automation, costs are reduced. The cost of administration of the purchasing department should be cut by 25-60%. Many companies will make similar savings in the generation and despatch of invoices. More difficult to quantify are the savings that stem from reductions in errors—typically down from 30% to 5%. These gains are there for the taking, but will come only after a thorough review and careful implementation of EDI—and they take time. EDI can be up and running in a small company in days, but it is not a technique that will bring instant cost reductions.

In the UK, the cost of each business document processed by paper— including the labour cost and overheads—is at least £10. With a 25% reduction in the cost, British industry could cut its costs by £12 billion a year. In the US, the cost of a business document is put at $30-50; one company at the top end of the scale found that documents sent by EDI cost only $15, a saving of 70%, and a company with lower overheads cut the cost of each document by 20%.

Certainly, a 25% reduction is a realistic target for EDI—and such targets are essential to any implementation programme. Obviously, in the short-term, there are additional costs in investment and training, and as with any new system, the long view must be taken.

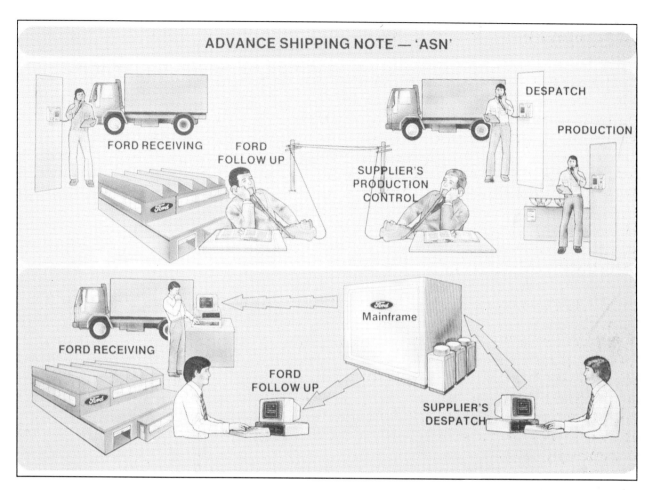

Fig. 10.1. Whereas several different telephone calls, each prone to error, are required to ascertain the progress with deliveries normally, one set of data is sent once by EDI

Savings of over 50%

Philips UK is one of the companies that has quantified the benefits of the use of EDI. It claims that the cost of incoming documents, such as invoices and delivery advice notes has been cut by 75%, and that the cost of orders and similar documents has been halved.

Cost reductions made by Philips UK with EDI

	Cost, £/1,000 documents		
	Manual	EDI	Saving, %
Incoming	1,510	325	78
Outgoing	110	55	50

By any standards this is a considerable gain, albeit made by a large company with international operations. Those gains came purely with the use of EDI for existing documents.

With the use of EDI, much paperwork disappears immediately. In the case of a manufacturer, several pieces of paper disappear altogether, to be replaced by digital data popping up on computer screens where needed. The documents taken out of the process are:

☐ Internal order to purchasing department;
☐ Purchase order;
☐ Purchase order acknowledgement;
☐ Internal sales order;
☐ Delivery advice note;
☐ Invoice;
☐ Remittance advice;
☐ Several envelopes and postage.

Self-billing cuts number of processes

Moreover, since self-billing replaces the issuing of invoices, the work required to raise the invoice has disappeared from the process altogether. The elimination of all this paperwork, and the people that are used to raise it, handle it, sort out queries, and errors and losses, results in a considerable reduction in overheads in any company.

Some managers may doubt whether the invoice can be pensioned off. However, the situation is little different from the change that has taken place in retailing over the past 20 years. Formerly, the customer would order goods from the grocer—either by telephone or verbally—and the grocer would make up the order and hand over an invoice. Then the customer would check the invoice against the goods and pay by cash or cheque, which the grocer would then take to the bank.

Now, the customer selects the goods from the shelves of the supermarket, and chooses substitutes for anything he or she does not find. In effect, the customer self-bills when he or she allows the items to be passed over the bar code scanner. With a direct debit by Switch, the cycle is completed without the need for the cheque or cash to be taken to the bank.

Self-billing has been operated in some industries for many years and, as long as the vendor has the opportunity of auditing stock levels and of contesting payments, is a reliable system. Of course, its success depends on trust between vendor and customer, but trust is in any case an essential ingredient in any business partnership.

Errors and hassle eliminated

In manufacturing, the reduction in transactions involved in the delivery of components by a vendor is dramatic. Traditionally, once the manufacturer has placed an order, progress chasers telephone the vendor's production controller regularly to ensure that the components will be delivered on time. The production controller contacts his own production department to check on progress, and reports back to the customer. Eventually, he will advise the customer that the components are ready for despatch, and the despatch department will then telephone the customer's goods receiving department to prepare them for a delivery. In each case, there is a good chance of an error being made in the part number, name, quantity or time of delivery. If the deliveries are not made regularly, the driver may even end up at the wrong plant or wrong gate. Every time, there is a one-in-three chance that an error will turn a routine delivery into shortages on the line, with telephone lines humming in all directions.

By contrast, with EDI, the customer informs the vendor when the delivery is to be made, the vendor's controller sends one set of data to the network, which is then read by both the progress chaser and goods receiving department. There is little room for error, since the data is based on that in the customer's original order, and a couple of EDI messages replace many telephone calls. Efficiency is therefore enhanced, costs cut, and relations with trading partners improved. Quite often, the use of EDI generates more business without any strategic changes being made by management.

Hard-headed accountants will appreciate the direct savings with EDI; with each business document that is eliminated the company's costs are cut by about £10. EDI pays off where companies usually find it most difficult to cut costs and maintain efficiency—administration. It is true that the cost of the EDI equipment, personnel and network replace some of the cost of paper, but some documents will not be replaced at all. In any case, as shown in Chapter One, people account for most of the cost of handling paperwork, and with EDI the headcount in accounts and purchasing departments can be reduced.

For example, ICI Chemicals found that its administrative operators spend 50% of their time inputting data, 25% correcting errors, and 25% in positive activities. It foresees that with EDI, 45% of the time spent can be made available for more creative activities. Other companies have found that the use of EDI has a similar effect on the sales department, enabling staff to spend more time generating new sales, and maintaining contacts with customers.

Integrate EDI for more gains

However, by integrating EDI into the full business cycle, manufacturers can cut costs further. For example, when the stock level at a manufacturer reaches a certain level, the fact can be relayed automatically to a terminal to trigger an automated procedure to order more. With the aid of a program to check the rate of use of the item, the order can be increased or reduced, and sent automatically, or flashed on to the display at the supervisor for examination.

Routine call-off orders can be sent straight to the network and on to the vendor. The vendor's computer can access the network to receive the order, and transfer the data to an in-house order to the plant. When the goods are available, their existence at the warehouse can be signalled by a bar code reader, and the necessary delivery instructions and delivery pre-notification can be sent to the customer. When the items are delivered, their receipt can be verified by bar code reader or by an operator, to trigger the confirmation of receipt and self-billing invoice. Not only is the paperwork eliminated, but most of the transactions required can be automated.

Reduced stocks

In almost any business, EDI will help reduce stock levels, bringing quantifiable benefits throughout the organisation. Once automated EDI trading is in operation, stock levels can be reduced. The co-operation of vendors, which will need to deliver smaller quantities more frequently, is needed, but the establishment of EDI links fosters such co-operation.

Overall, EDI can be a big cost-saver, as long as the implementation is thorough, and a long-term view is taken of the equipment, systems and personnel levels. It is therefore an essential ingredient in lean manufacture, while more will be gained arising from the way the company does business—the strategic changes. But operational changes need to be made first.

Chapter Eleven

EDI paves the way to lean production

EDI to 20% of partners cuts paperwork by 60%

Merge administration departments

Reduce stock levels and size of plants

EVEN in the booming 1980s it was recognised that to achieve world-class standards of quality and return on investment, manufacturers needed to emulate the Japanese and become lean. Now that prospects for sustained growth are less certain while competition is increasing, the need to slim down is even more urgent. There is no alternative but to strive to achieve lean production.

Recessions that require businesses to be pared down are nothing new, but in the past the absence of tools to remove the fat, resulted in some essential staff being made redundant along with those that were genuinely surplus to requirements. Often, people were made redundant because they were non-productive, with production control being a typical target for the hatchet men. Initially, the run-down in production would mask the inefficiency that resulted, but once there was the slightest upturn in demand, control would become sloppy, stocks would rise, and shortages would reappear. Yet fearful of a further downturn, management would resist the call for extra staff. Only when production was running flat out, and shortages were a major problem, would extra staff be brought in—and usually that would have been not long before the next downturn in demand.

Better control, lower administrative costs

With an integrated approach to EDI, management can have the best of both worlds: it can reduce administrative staff and improve control of stock. To do so, however, the company needs to review its business thoroughly and introduce EDI as part of an improvement strategy, as discussed in Chapter Eleven. The hurried introduction of EDI as a move to control deliveries and reduce inventory in the goods receiving stores will not achieve the expected results—especially if it is introduced at the same time that staff are being made redundant.

However, once EDI is operating smoothly—initially for invoices, and later for the stages of the delivery process—there will be a need for fewer people in some departments, and a programme for reducing the size and manning levels can be planned. Meanwhile, the advent of EDI will allow managers to spend more of their time on core activities, instead of:

☐ Shuffling paperwork;
☐ Signing authorisations for changes to documents;
☐ Explaining to staff why a certain invoice does not match the delivery note, and what must be done;
☐ Chasing late deliveries, or deliveries temporarily lost in the black hole between the vendor's despatch department and the goods receiving stores.

Significant gains can be made with the use of EDI to trade with a small proportion of vendors or customers only. If a company trades electronically with about 20% of its vendors or customers—obviously with the larger ones in terms of the number of transactions and value—it will eliminate over 60% of the paperwork, which will have a dramatic effect on all aspects of administration.

Almost error-free

The differences in the environments of offices before and after EDI are dramatic. Now, there are errors in only 3-5% of invoices, against 30% in the days of paper. Therefore, 80% of the time formerly spent rejecting invoices with errors and chasing up corrections is available for more productive work. For example, Texas Instruments now sends 60% of its orders by EDI, so that 150,000 orders a year are sent without human intervention. Previously, about 600 orders would have been keyed into a computer, checked, printed out and authorised every day; now no people are required for this work. The effect of such a change can only be described as dramatic.

At Digital Equipment, the purchasing officers spend only two hours a week with paperwork, against 25 hours previously; now they can spend that time improving relations with vendors, finding how the vendor can cut costs and improve quality, and looking for new materials— in other words, doing the job they are actually paid to do.

Hewlett Packard's German operation found similar benefits with EDI; it saved 25-40% of its buyers' time. Previously, administrative errors in taking orders, or in the order being placed incorrectly, also led to substantial amounts of materials being returned to the vendor. With EDI, the amount of material returned has been cut by 35-45%, reducing transport and administrative costs. Changes of this magnitude do not reduce costs only; they raise morale and make people much more positive about their work.

Toward lean production

Once critical mass is achieved with EDI, there is scope for considerable streamlining of administrative operations. Offices will begin to look idle, as people sit at their desks controlling operations instead of chasing a manager or colleague for a missing piece of information. Next, it will become apparent that smaller departments with fewer people will be able to do the job. Then will come the opportunity to consider whether all those separate, traditional departments are needed. Perhaps they can be

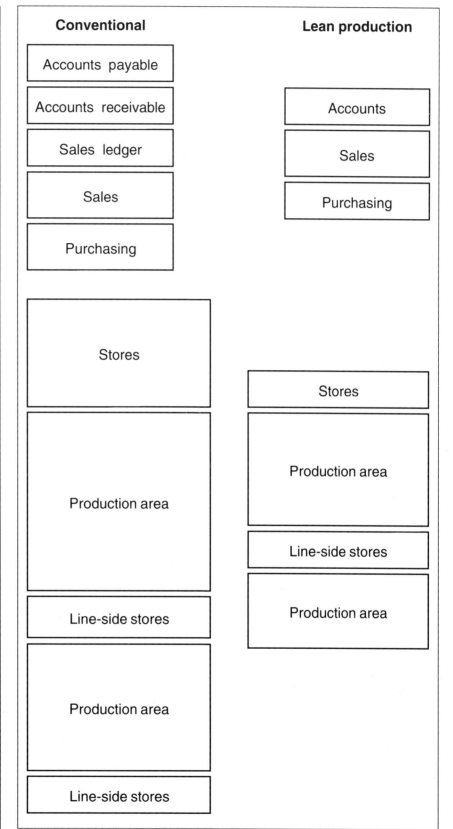

Fig. 11.1. With the combination of EDI, JIT and kanban systems, lean production, which requires less space and fewer administration departments, becomes a reality

merged with a further gain in efficiency. However, the same number of key personnel will be needed, and care is needed in making redundancies. In many cases, the streamlining will lead to an increase in business so that the redundant staff can be employed elsewhere.

The next key to streamlining comes with the combination of EDI and JIT—both inside the factory and to control deliveries from vendors. Immediately EDI is in use, seven to ten days are cut from the lead time required by vendors. Owing to the inevitable delay with paper trading, a factory making 100 assemblies a week, each consisting of 100 components, requires a minimum stock at the moment when a replacement order is placed of seven days' production—140 sets or a total of 14,000 components. In practice, the minimum would be around 20,000 components, but production managers would add a 25-50% safety margin. On top of that, inevitable inefficiencies in stock control and buffers would add more components to the normal level. Therefore, the minimum stock level before JIT and EDI would probably be 40,000 components, or a month's production.

Less lead time, less stock

The reduction in the cycle by seven to ten days should be exploited with an immediate reduction in stock and with later orders, so that the accuracy of the quantities and timing can be improved. Flushing out the unnecessary stock held in the plant—one interpretation of JIT is that the volume of stock is replaced by the volume of information—will lead to the leanness common in Japan.

Because of fewer errors in quantities and specification that come with EDI and the use of special-purpose returnable pallets instead of disposable packaging, manufacturers will have greater confidence that components and materials will always be at the production line when needed. With JIT, there are more frequent deliveries of smaller lots, all of which lead to less space being required in the goods receiving stores, and in the workshops.

However, space released in this change should not be left empty. Such empty spaces tend to demoralise the employees who feel they are working in a mere shadow of the former plant, where every corner was stacked with components. And there will be a temptation for people to place defective assemblies or extra components in the empty spaces.

It is necessary therefore to make sweeping changes once it is decided that stocks can be reduced by 50%, for example. Immediately, the area devoted to the stores must be reduced, and preferably replaced with compact automatic storage and retrieval racking. Next, the workshops need to be rearranged so that all sequential production operations are much closer together than formerly, so that the distance workpieces must cover between sections is reduced. Small racks, with space for a few pallets only, should be placed at the assembly lines. Where volumes are low, kits of parts may be provided on trolleys that move with or carry the assembly, so there may be racks for standard items such as fasteners only at the stations.

With this sort of operation, which will result in improved morale in the plants, some space will be redundant. Whether this is sold or earmarked for new products, for product development or a pilot build shop will depend on the company. But it should not be left idle, a drag on overheads.

Savings equal 7-10% increase in sales

At the other end of the business, the use of EDI will speed up the issuing and transmission of invoices. Therefore, the use of EDI will enable a manufacturer to cut costs in two ways:

☐ By reducing stock;
☐ By cutting the time waiting for invoices to be paid.

A manufacturer should be able to reduce the amount of stock from 25 days' sales to at least 17 days with EDI alone. With a little more effort made to reduce surplus stock, and with JIT deliveries, a reduction of another five days should be practical—in other words, a reduction in stock of 50%.

At the same time, the improved invoicing should result in the average waiting period for payment from 60 to 55 days. In the case of a company with a turnover of £10 million a year, data compiled by Compument Software shows that with these changes:

☐ The capital tied up in stock would be reduced from £1,000,000 to £500,000;

☐ The interest on that capital at 15% would be reduced by £75,000;

☐ The capital tied up by debtors would be reduced from £1.64 million to £1.5 million;

☐ The interest on the capital would be reduced by £20,000;

☐ Pre-tax profits would be increased by £95,000, or 8%, the equivalent of an increase in sales of £790,000.

An increase in sales of that amount may come in a booming market, but with an increase in inventory and administrative costs, so the benefits with these reductions are greater than with extra sales. In a difficult environment, the reduction in overdraft could be a key to survival, and in any circumstances would be very welcome. Yet the achievements are very modest. With a systematic approach to the reduction of stock throughout the plant by EDI and JIT, the capital tied up in stock could be cut further. A small part of those funds might be needed to fund the changes in the plant to maximise the benefits of JIT and *Kanban* systems, but would yield an excellent return.

Bar codes to route components

One other area where administration can be streamlined is with the aid of bar code labels discussed in Chapter Nine. Their use can cut the cost of goods receiving and should also be exploited where practical in routing components through the plant. Automated guided vehicles, which can be cost-effective even in small plants, are an aid here.

Another area where EDI allows fat to be cut is in transport. Currently, once a consignment is loaded on to a carrier's truck for shipment to a customer, it enters a black hole, only to re-emerge when the goods are

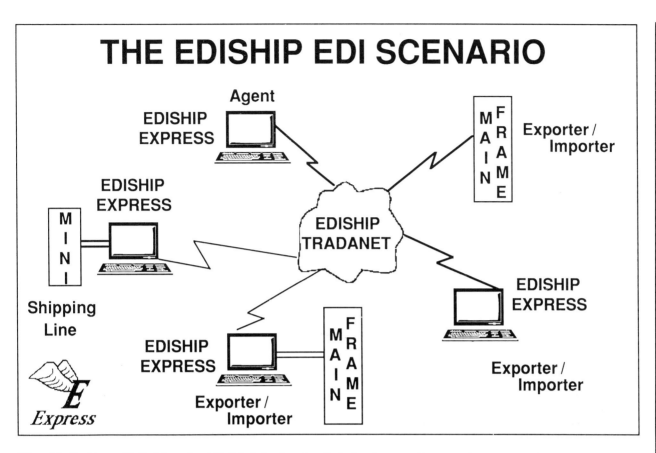

Fig. 11.2. Once Ediship, the EDI initiative in freight forwarding and shipping, or similar schemes are used by shippers worldwide, manufacturers will be able to reduce transport costs and the time their goods spend in transit

delivered. With EDI, the carrier will be able to notify both vendor and customer of the time of receipt at its warehouse or docks, or arrival in the country of the customer, if appropriate, and indeed at any point when the consignment is stationary. Not only does this give both trading partners greater confidence in each other, but also it makes comparisons between the performance of different carriers more precise. No excuses can be made about traffic jams or delays at Customs or ports, since the idle time will be known. The irony of this situation is that because of this inefficiency, the haulier requires large warehouses, which are effectively financed by users. Once hauliers start to streamline with EDI, the cost of transport should be reduced.

EDI is already in use by a number of hauliers, while the Ediship initiative is intended to spread EDI throughout the shipping and freight forwarding industry. Users of Ediship will soon account for over 90% of all deep sea cargo to and from the UK. The need for this initiative is indicated by the fact that a typical international shipment may involve 27 organisations, 40 original documents and 360 copies. Paperwork, 30% of which is related solely to transport, accounts for 7-10% of the final price of the product. With EDI, there must be scope for cutting that on-cost in half.

No human intervention

For the greatest operational benefits from EDI itself, the system needs to be integrated into existing applications software. For example, when an order is received from the customer, it should be routed directly from the EDI gateway (See Chapter Eight) into the order processing software in the sales department without any human intervention. The existence of the order should be flagged, or drawn to the attention of the computer operator, only if necessary. Ideally, the operator will be discouraged by the way the program operates from doing anything other than send that order through to production.

A menu should indicate whether the order is a routine call-off order, or a special, or one needing sales attention. In the case of a call-off order, the operator needs merely to ensure that the order is accurate—largely automatically—and that it is sent through to the relevant systems, preferably in an automatic transaction. In other cases, some action may be needed, but the document should not be printed out unless it is essential—people need to be encouraged to work without paper.

As soon as production receives the order, it will need to investigate its schedule and stock levels to ascertain that it can meet the customer's requirement. These actions also can be automated, leaving the manager to assess the results and indicate the delivery date quickly.

Therefore, with the full use of EDI, manufacture can be streamlined in a number of ways:

☐ Administration costs are reduced;
☐ Stock levels in goods receiving and work-in-progress can be cut substantially, freeing up capital and increasing overall efficiency;
☐ Many manual processes can be automated;
☐ The company can respond more quickly to orders;
☐ Relations with vendors and customers can be improved.

For some managers, these gains will seem sufficient, and they will certainly take some time to achieve. However, they are just the start. Next comes a reshaping of the business, with new opportunities being grasped.

Chapter Twelve

Gateway to new business

EDI and simultaneous engineering weld supply chain into flexible, efficient resource

Market worldwide, to new business sectors

Cross-marketing deals

ONCE EDI is operating smoothly, management will receive more up-to-date information about several aspects of its business, and will be in a position to rethink strategies. It is here that EDI becomes an enabling technology, allowing management to make changes it would not have considered feasible a few years ago. EDI is concerned with adding value, not with cutting costs.

First, since administration can be smaller there is a case for some internal restructuring. Are all these departments, set up when administration revolved around information being logged by pen and ink actually needed? Or could they all be handled by one administration department, providing a service to the main functions? Could some of those operations, which are on the fringe of the company's operations, be handled better by an outside specialist? For example, there was a time when major manufacturers had large departments to handle insurance. Such a department, removed from the mainstream activities of the company, and from the mainstream of the insurance world could neither be efficient nor up-to-date. It is preferable to find some specialist brokers who can quote for a long-term contract, and become part of the team.

In the workshops, managers can reassess the potential for reaching the goal of a batch of one, or for large volume manufacture, the batch of 30 with 15-20 different items in each batch. Flexible manufacture will not only be feasible, but successful, and there is the opportunity to integrate the supply chain from materials to components to finished assembly into a continuous process—with a comprehensive system to chase the inevitable defects so that damages can be contained. There is plenty of scope for EDI on the customer side too, to trigger automatic orders, to transmit information to dealers and to seek out new business.

Increases flexibility

As is well-known, the inescapable trend in the marketplace is for customers to demand greater variety, resulting in smaller batches. This is in direct opposition to production's aim for big volumes to reduce costs. The answers to these conundrums lie in more flexible manufacture, not only in-house but also by vendors—a flexible supply chain. Flexibility throughout the supply chain will come only with an integrated system in which all partners recognise that they are committed to the success of the ultimate product. To achieve the high level of performance and the sense of teamwork, manufacturers need to help their vendors operate flexibly in the same way that they do themselves.

Little is gained with the adoption of flexible manufacturing equipment and the cutting of stock levels by 50% in-house only for the vendor to continue to operate outmoded automation equipment to produce large batches, drawing stock from a huge warehouse at short notice to match customers' requirements. The result will be very large inventory costs with many potential problems of poor quality and damage.

At best, the customer pays for that inventory, but at worst a quick shift to a new product in response to falling demand for an old one will lead to serious problems. The vendor will want to dispose of a huge amount of stock, for which it will expect to be paid, and will scrap some automation equipment. If the customer wriggles out of paying for the stock and retooling, it will pay for it in one way or another: perhaps in higher prices, or in less co-operation in new projects, but possibly with the vendor being forced out of business at a critical phase in one of the customer's new projects.

Simultaneous engineering the key

By adopting EDI and giving their vendors plenty of accurate information, manufacturers will improve relations. But they need to go further: to speed up their own new product development, leading manufacturers are adopting simultaneous engineering*.

Not only does this approach reduce time-to-market —usually by 20-40%—but it results in products that match customers' requirements, improved quality,

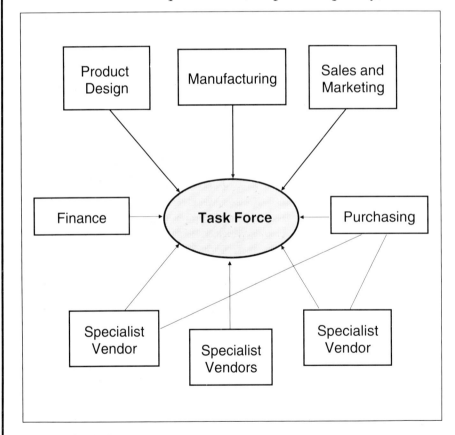

Fig. 12.1. The key to successful simultaneous engineering is the combination of multi-disciplinary teams with the use of specific design tools, such as Quality Function Deployment

*See 'Simultaneous Engineering: The management Guide' (2nd Edition) published by Industrial Newsletters Ltd, Tel: 05255 2060, for details of the tremendous benefits of this technique

reduced costs and allows the company to be more responsive to the market. It is no wonder, therefore, that EDI and simultaneous engineering are combined in the DoD's CALS initiative.

Once simultaneous engineering teams are set up, representatives of the main vendors of manufacturing equipment and components are brought into the team. The process of quotations for a contract after the design has been completed is replaced by a system in which vendors are selected before the design is started for specific contracts on the basis of their general level of technology, price competitiveness, and attention to whole-life costs.

Immediately, one big area of conflict is removed from the vendor-manufacturer relationship: who pays for modifications made during the programme, and how much. The payment is discussed by the team with the vendor, and the sharing of costs is agreed on the basis of mutual confidence and shared information.

With simultaneous engineering, the vendors, who are gaining confidence in their business relationship with the manufacturer through the EDI links, will find another cause of friction with the customer disappears. Co-operation increases to such an extent that the supply chain will approach that seamless ideal—from design onward. Needless to say, the path to full EDI and simultaneous engineering relationships are not without their pitfalls and problems. However, these are essential tools for any company attempting to achieve world class.

CADCAM data

Ultimately, CADCAM data will be transferred between partners in the chain by EDI, both at the development stages and for production tooling, but at present the preferred method of transfer is by magnetic tape. The transmission of data for a three-dimensional CAD model of a component can take several hours at present rates of transfer, so until data compression is combined with high-speed lines, it is not practical on a routine basis. In any case, data for tooling is not sent frequently. On the other hand, for full interactive design between manufacturer and vendor, ultra-high speed transfer is essential. Then, designers in two or three different locations will be able to design the same component together simultaneously—a multi-location design session to parallel the video conference being adopted by multi-national companies for business meetings.

JIT and minimal downtime

On the manufacturing front, the use of flexible equipment to produce small batches will be complemented by the use of EDI between partners in the supply chain, and in-house to speed-up the delivery of small batches. Typical of the approach of those seeking world-class quality and lean production is Mitel Manufacturing Technologies which adopted cell manufacture, EDI to control deliveries from vendors and a *kanban* system to control in-house stocks. As a result it cut the lead time for its products from 58 to five days. It was also able to reduce the lead time for components from vendors from around 80 days to 40 days, and is now heading for 25 days.

As mentioned in earlier chapters, JIT itself is not enough to achieve world class. It is also important to eliminate unnecessary downtime when tools are changed to allow the production of different components or assemblies. In fact, this is just one aspect of the elimination of waste that is essential in any attempt to adopt lean production. Other types of waste are:

☐ Over-production to produce stock;
☐ The production of rejects;
☐ The manufacture of products with features the customer does not require;
☐ Scrap raw materials, such as offcuts discarded when blanks are cut and risers from diecastings;
☐ Resources, such as water, that is wasted rather than being recycled;
☐ Machines or people that are underutilised.

It is simple enough to produce flexible assembly cells in which the downtime between batches is minimal. Robots can be installed with interchangeable grippers and multiple parts feeders, so that several different components can be handled without downtime between batches. Then, multi-purpose pallets can be used to carry different chassis along the line.

Where standard equipment is in use, the solution cannot be bought; instead, procedures need to be changed. For example, to reduce the batch sizes sufficiently to suit the market without increasing costs, it is necessary to be able to change tools very quickly in many machines. Typical of the requirements are to:

☐ Change dies in a 500-800 tonne press in 10 minutes;
☐ Change dies in an aluminium diecasting machine or injection moulding machine in 5-10 minutes;
☐ Change the gear set in Gleason gear cutting machines in less than 15 minutes.

In these examples, the time quoted represents loss of production, not the time the men are working on the machine. In most plants, these jobs take from four to eight hours, so the production of a batch for one shift is uneconomic. The key to success in this area is in rethinking the job so that about 90% of the operations are performed in the tool shop, with the minimum amount of work being done at the machine when it is stopped. Also, it is necessary to provide two cranes at the diecasting or injection moulding machine, one to carry the new dies, and the other to remove the old ones. Such improvements may be far removed from EDI, but are needed for flexible manufacture to be profitable.

Sharing gains with vendor

With changes such as these, manufacturers are able to streamline production as never before; and control the processes of their vendors. Their manufacturing engineers should work with those of vendors to improve flow through the plants and to reduce downtime between batches. The result will be an improvement in efficiency for all.

How do companies ensure that the gains are divided between the members of the supply chain? Xerox is one company that has attempted to ensure that this happens in what it calls the co-operative contracting approach. It starts with the assumption that at the beginning and end

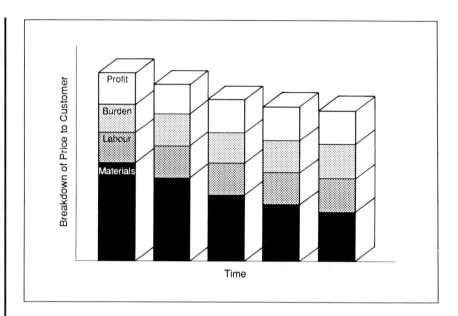

Fig. 12.2. Xerox established its co-operative contracts scheme to ensure that vendors made efforts to reduce costs yet received a fair profit margin

of the production run, the vendor should receive a profit margin of 15%. In addition, it expects the vendor to be able to reduce the price several times during that period—these are long-term contracts, of course.

At the same time, Xerox expects all the constituent costs—overheads, labour and materials—to be reduced, but not necessarily in equal steps or at the same time. A reduction in materials costs can come from improved sourcing, a change in specification, or a reduction in the mass of the product from a change in design. This is a model technique that strengthens the supply chain so long as the customer and vendor work together to reduce costs and improve quality—obviously it will not work if all the vendor's requests for changes are met with the negative response endemic in the old-fashioned approach to vendors engendered by sequential engineering and multiple sourcing.

With this new approach, in which the whole supply chain from raw materials to the sales outlet receives attention, manufacturers will convert a group of vendors into a supply chain. They will recognise that the supply chain is only as strong as its weakest link, and act accordingly. At the same time, they will be able to integrate activities, so that the suppliers of materials to a component maker are just as much part of the chain as the vendor of sub-assemblies. Automation of routine activities will enable people to turn their attention to improving the supply chain itself.

More information for dealers

EDI also has a role to play between the manufacturer and dealer or final customer. GM's Saturn Corporation has taken the lead here in interrogating and controlling the stock levels at dealers automatically. In this way, shortages of new cars or replacement parts at dealerships are eliminated, raising the overall standard of service to customers. EDI can also be used to transmit:

☐ Changes to prices;
☐ Changes to specification;
☐ Information concerning recalls or faulty parts;
☐ New parts manuals;
☐ New service manuals.

To reinforce pure EDI, live video shows can be broadcast to dealers so that they can see new product launches, and video conferences can be held with key personnel. These moves bring them closer to the manufacturer, and will lay the groundwork for increased sales, particularly since several people employed at each dealer will be freed from tedious paperwork.

Small manufacturers sell worldwide

With EDI, the whole world becomes the oyster of not just the large manufacturer, but of the small vendor as well. The message to all users of EDI is: Think globally.

Once a company has made contact with a potential vendor or customer in a remote country, it will be able to send requests for quotations or offers of components in the clear knowledge that the EDI-capable recipient will be able to understand the message. The foreign company may need to translate the description of the part into its own language, but everything else will be clear, owing to the use of standard data fields.

In addition, the two partners will recognise common EDI messages, so EDI will transcend barriers not just of language but also of different cultures. Therefore, long-distance international trade will grow.

Partly owing to the increase in international trade, but also to keep greater control of their businesses, managers will need to eliminate time wasted in the transport cycle. With full auditing of the transport trail, EDI will enable comparisons between different freight forwarders and shipping lines to be made, leading to the use of the most efficient ones only. The need for greater efficiency in transport, well known to managers, is demonstrated by a survey which showed that air freight spends 92% of the time in transit on the ground. The opportunities for increased efficiency are clearly substantial in all forms of transport.

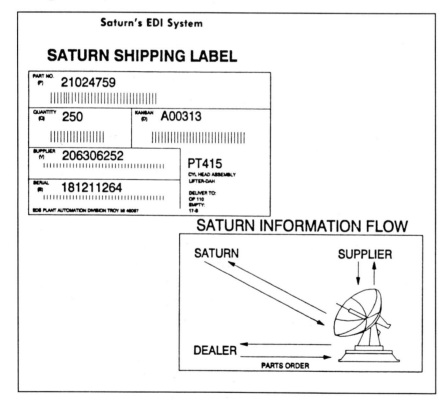

Fig. 12.3. GM's Saturn Corporation uses a satellite EDI system to transfer data to vendors and dealers. The relevant data are printed on to shipping labels by the vendors

But where is the new business? To start with, once a company is EDI-capable, any manufacturer or retailer using EDI becomes a potential customer, and one that will have a system of procedures very similar to those of the vendor. For example, vendors that previously did not want to supply the retail business, will find that with EDI they will be able to deal readily with the biggest retail chains. Since the trend is for these chains to take a bigger slice of the overall market, growth in that business should follow.

Quicker response, cross-marketing deal

Also, with EDI throughout the chain, companies will be able to respond more quickly to changes in fashion in their market, therefore increasing market share. These days, fashion is an aspect of almost all consumer products, even those with long lives.

Small companies may find that with EDI it becomes practical to market complementary products of other companies, and thus offer potential customers wider services. For example, a diecaster could market the services of toolmakers or of a jobbing machine shop; a gear maker could market the services of a diecaster or forge; an injection moulder could market plastics sheet, inserts, handling equipment for moulding or casting machines, or dies or die castings. There are large numbers of potential alliances that would strengthen the individual companies without harming the core businesses; these would be alliances, based primarily on the exchange of data, and not mergers which create far too many problems for small companies.

Large companies can also market products they do not make, since EDI allows the necessary data to be as up-to-date as that of the maker. There is already a trend in this direction, with some unusual marketing alliances in small sectors.

In addition, a new breed of finance companies is likely to be set up by manufacturers. Although these will handle credit contracts, some will also make arrangements with vendors, dealers and some equivalent companies to handle remittances. Companies would interchange details of their balances with each other and make periodical balancing credits so that the actual transfer of funds would take place less frequently than normal. Thus, banking charges and administration would be cut.

Those manufacturers that deal directly with the public could make arrangements for clients and employees to cash cheques—with on-line verification at the bank so that the amount of cash handled would be reduced further.

Customised books

As mentioned earlier, demand for customised products will increase in the future, opening up new markets for nimble companies. For example, McGraw-Hill, finding that many heads of faculties at American universities were not satisfied with its textbooks, started to market a service to provide customised textbooks. The professor or group interrogates the database of textbooks on a particular subject and chooses which sections of which books it requires. It then places an order for the new composite textbook, and thanks to a fast printing and binding system, McGraw-Hill can deliver 100 copies of the book within three-four days. Clearly, neither the EDI element nor the fast printing system would be any advantage alone; both were needed to open the new business.

This is typical of how business can be increased. Another opportunity comes directly with the advent of EDI: companies will want to spread their net further when looking for components and services. Therefore, demand for databases of engineering materials, fasteners, components and stock levels at metals stockholders is certain to increase. Some companies may be able to use the data they are collecting to offer a database service. Also, there are clearly opportunities for new concepts, such as a warehouse/catalogue vendor of products and materials to engineering companies based entirely on EDI.

We are entering the era of information, and manufacturers need to be mindful they can profit from the information they hold, and do not end up paying for information they could sell directly, or that would help them sell products. For example, a manufacturer involved in one industry might be able to exchange data with one in another to avoid paying for the data from a network.

Exploit information to find new business

Extra business can come from the exploitation of information. For example, a vendor operating in one industry only, might find that many of the components and materials it uses are required by another industry that is more fragmented. It could establish a new company or division to market surface finishes, materials, fasteners, electrical equipment and other products to the other industry, obtaining the necessary information from its database. In some cases, the extra volume might lead to lower prices for its main business, while it could profit directly from the new activities.

EDI is a means of obtaining and disseminating information. It enables companies to enter new sectors of business, because they now have the necessary data they can convert into valuable information. It is therefore a very powerful technology, enabling users to:

☐ Improve the efficiency of their administration;
☐ Streamline their business by reducing stock levels and lead times;
☐ Convert a group of suppliers into a supply chain;
☐ Give more information to their retail outlets;
☐ Open up new markets and business opportunities.

Some of these new areas of business will be extensions of the existing sphere of operations, such as a contract with a retail chain or to supply an overseas manufacturer. Others will involve the use of EDI to encourage new customers to buy a company's products rather than use their traditional channels. Elsewhere companies will be able to market products they do not make themselves. Meanwhile, the involvement in IT could lead to the marketing of new services such as databases. The opportunities expand as EDI develops.

Chapter Thirteen

Putting EDI to work

Review business processes first

Legal and administrative considerations

Big, volatile orders best for first routine use

BEFORE becoming involved with EDI, a company needs to look inward; to buy some hardware and software and move straight into a pilot programme is a recipe for disaster. Nor is it sufficient to start with a review of the paperwork. First comes an assessment of the company itself; then the review of the paperwork and data flow; and only then does EDI itself come into the picture.

Clearly, for any changes to be made in the business strategy, senior management must be completely behind the move. In a large company, the initiative will probably come from lower in the hierarchy, and the managers involved need to find out something of their company before they promote EDI. First, they need to audit the culture to find the level of resistance to change. Key questions are:

☐ How much support is there for the managers making changes in the company?

☐ How many layers of management will be involved?

☐ What is extent of the resistance to change? This should be measured in the form of a rating.

Managers need to know how receptive to change the directors are, and only then will they be able to judge how far and how fast they can move with EDI. If the directors are very conservative, then the changes EDI will bring about will be accepted only at the operational level—a reduction in paperwork and headcount. If the Board is highly responsive to change, then it can be persuaded that EDI should be used as an instrument to change the way the company does business.

EDI champion

At this stage, an EDI champion, who should not be one of the IT staff, can be found. He or she needs natural enthusiasm for what EDI can do, and must be prepared to lead the project, but not necessarily as project manager. This individual will have the job of persuading the Board why EDI should be adopted, using non-technical terms. Once the Board has given its support to EDI, it is necessary to see how receptive others are to change. For example, how big is the technology gap? Is there any interest in handling new technology? Or do people equate technology with complication, problems, and unwelcome change in working practices without any benefits?

In a small company, the initiative is likely to come from a director, and he or she will need to persuade the other directors that EDI is an essential plank in any future strategy. The low cost of EDI equipment should not be used as a lever to gain management's acquiescence, however. Instead, the emphasis should be placed on the total benefits. Once the potential has been recognised, the need to train people to maximise the benefits can be brought out.

Eventually, the EDI champion will overcome the initial hurdles, and will agree an EDI strategy with senior managers. It will include quantified targets and a timetable. In any project, targets are needed to focus people's minds on what they can achieve, and produce results that can be publicised to gain the interest of people not involved in the project.

At this stage the strategy is unlikely to be firm, simply because it takes time for people to grasp the potential of a new technique. However, long-term targets should be set at this stage, to be reviewed periodically.

EDI will change the company

It is also important to consider how EDI will change the company. There is a well-defined path for major changes involving technology. It starts with awareness of the new technology, and then the awareness of the changes that will be required. After that, the expected changes need to be understood by those involved. Next comes the promotional phase, where a positive perception needs to be fostered, and any negative thoughts eliminated. In due course, the new system is installed, and later on it is accepted. Finally, the change becomes institutionalised so any gains will be marginal. By that time, it is likely that a substantial number of employees will have joined the company after the introduction of the technology, so to them it is just part of the structure.

Clearly, when the EDI champion encounters any danger signals at each stage he or she needs to recognise them and act accordingly. For example, until people are aware that change is needed, it is fruitless to promote the

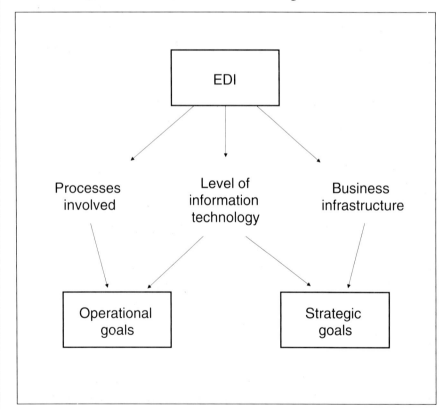

Fig. 13.1. EDI involves many facets of a business and its technologies. Operational and strategic goals are necessary for success

technology; the move will lead to resistance being built up. Equally, the time to push for maximum change is when acceptance is coming—if left too late, the technology will become institutionalised, and people will not accept anything other than minor changes to 'their system'.

Multi-disciplinary project team

Once this pattern of change is recognised, an EDI project team with members drawn from different departments should be set up. Its first job will be to review the paperwork and data flow in the company and between it and its main trading partners. The multi-disciplinary team is needed for any technology involving change; without it, the benefits will not be realised fully. In many cases opposition from departments not involved have torpedoed the best-laid plans for change.

Although the review of paperwork is conducted with an eye to electronic transmissions, the first aim should be to simplify the documents and eliminate redundant information, or information that is included just because it always has been.

The ultimate aim with EDI is not to simplify documents, however; it is to obliterate them from use.

Learning about EDI

To gain information on EDI, some of the team will attend public conferences, and will contact the network operators to obtain details of the services and lists of users. Then, they will talk to some potential partners to discuss their aims in using EDI. It is clearly important that major partners be responsive to change, and prepared to adopt new methods.

At the same time, the team should hold brainstorming sessions at which ways of streamlining the business with EDI are discussed.

At this stage the team will need to decide on its approach to the IT aspects of the project. Should the software be developed in house? Should consultants be used? As discussed in Chapter Eight, there is little point in developing software for translation or communications in-house, but if there is a substantial IT department, it may pay to write software to link different applications together.

On the other hand, small companies, with little IT experience would do well to use an EDI consultant, at least to help them choose software and prepare it for use. A member of 'the company' should be involved in any decision over software or hardware, however, because in the end it is 'the company' that has to operate it and eliminate snags, not the consultant.

At least one medium-size company thought it had sufficient computer-literate management to install the software and set it up to suit its requirements, but after spending several days at the job the firm was obliged to call in a consultant. It is far better to call one in at the beginning, even if this is for a very limited amount of work.

Incidentally, whenever a consultant is called in, the job brief needs to be written clearly and precisely in some detail. It must be made clear that he or she is concerned with this work only. Of course, the consultant may see other areas where with a little work, it is possible to improve operations. But such ideas should not even be discussed until the job for which he or she was commissioned has been completed satisfactorily.

Alternatively, some members of staff can be sent on courses. Among the training centres for EDI is Langton College, Henley-on-Thames, set up specifically to run EDI courses developed by Langton Ltd in association with SITPRO.

Start-up and running costs

An alternative approach is to use the VAN operator as a consultant. For example, INS offers a package deal to new subscribers which includes the Intercept or Intercept-Plus software, training and registration as a subscriber for around £5,000.

The cost of INS's service thereafter consists of an annual fee of £1,000, irrespective of size, which tends to penalise the small user. Transmission charges are 21p/message plus 4-6p/1,000 characters transmitted. Overall charges for short messages are therefore high.

AT&T Istel recently adopted a new price structure with a nominal annual subscription of £20. The transmission fee is 10p/1,000 characters subject to a minimum charge of £50/month. New subscribers pay a set-up charge of £230. The software package, still named Edict PC, which has a full range of features including the ability to send several messages in one batch, costs £1,650.

A typical EDI invoice contains about 250 characters, so the transmission cost is about 22p by Tradanet and 2.5p by AT&T EDI. In practice, the small user, sending 1,000 documents a year will pay INS approximately £1,225, and AT&T Istel the minimum of £620 a year. A company with an output of 10,000 documents a year will pay INS £3,250, and AT&T Istel £620; for 100,000 documents a year, equivalent figures are £23,000 and £2,500 respectively.

Even INS subscribers will recoup the cost of postage with an output of about 15,000 documents a year—300/week. Moreover, if the vendor's customers operate a self-billing system, the reduced cost of invoicing will more than pay for the cost of the VAN.

Legal aspects

Before the team advances too far, the auditor should be consulted over the legal aspects of EDI. Generally, to satisfy the auditor, the electronic data must be saved securely, and must be capable of being printed out in an intelligible form. It must be complete, and not diverted, and the recipient must treat it as securely as the sender. Any transfer, such as an order, needs authorisation, and the level of authorisation should be defined.

A data interchange agreement between partners is also essential. Various bodies have devised models, and most follow the code of conduct laid down by the UNCID committee, which included representatives from the International Chamber of Commerce, SITPRO, Odette, the EC and the Customs Co-operation Council. The EDI Association is one body that has produced an interchange agreement and manuals specific to various trades.

It is also important to ascertain the moment at which a document is deemed to have been sent and received. There is a precedent with telex messages which are deemed to have been received when they are sent, and this seems appropriate for EDI. If self-billing is to be adopted, the point at which goods are deemed to have been purchased also needs to be agreed. With JIT deliveries, the point of acceptance is likely to be when the goods are received—preferably when the bar code of the pallet is scanned, and the quantity confirmed by a storeman— or it may be when they are delivered to the production line. (The use of bar codes is discussed in Chapter Nine.)

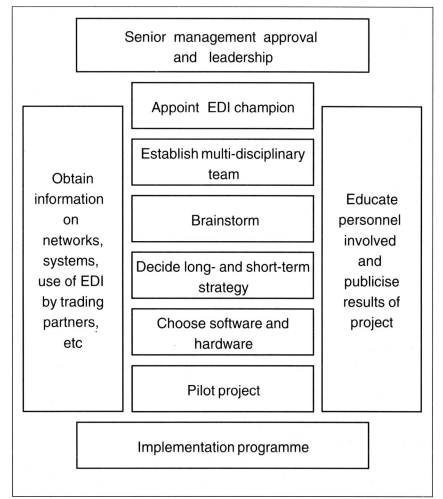

Fig. 13.2. Key steps in an EDI programme include selection of an EDI champion and a multi-disciplinary team, a strategic plan, education and a pilot project

First document, first partner

With this groundwork performed, the team can set up its basic programme, and look for the first documents and partners. The document will almost certainly be either the invoice or the purchase order; if the first partner is a large customer, it is likely to request the invoice first, not least because 'sender pays all' in EDI, so it does not incur any costs.

More care is needed in the selection of the first trading partner, which needs to be receptive to change, ready for teething troubles to occur in the early days; preferably it is one already using EDI. However, this first partner will be involved in a pilot project, and need not be one of the first partners with whom full-scale EDI is desirable; it could be chosen on the basis of its enthusiasm and flexibility. Once the pilot project has proved a success—it will continue until it is—a major business partner could be chosen in the knowledge that the system will work.

Normally, paper documents are sent in parallel with EDI messages for the first stage of the pilot project. For the first transmission, the normal document is sent by mail, which has the effect of creating enthusiasm for EDI as people wait around for the paper invoice to arrive in the post. Once that stage has passed, it is better to send the hard copy by fax, so that the waiting time is eliminated.

When error-free transmissions are being made, EDI is used alone, but the document is printed out on receipt and used as a paper document from then on. At this stage, it must be emphasised to all involved that this is not real EDI, but a temporary measure to help them gain confidence in the new system, and to iron out bugs. When people have gained sufficient confidence in the system, the data can be transferred to the applications software without any rekeying of data or printing.

Start with large but volatile quantities

Most big users of EDI have started with a major supplier, and have aimed to trade electronically with the companies that supply them with the largest volume or value of components. However, this is not necessarily the best approach. In the short term, the aim is to eliminate paperwork, so EDI is ideal for orders for small lots, which create many invoices, call-off orders, and delivery advice notes. In fact, the actual value of the orders may not be high, but the cost of the paperwork certainly is.

EDI shows biggest gains where there is a combination of large volume of business with big fluctuations in demand, such as in fashion goods of all types, and optional equipment on cars. Normally, larger fluctuations in demand lead to frequent shortages, so the progress chasers spend a disproportionate amount of their time chasing these components. However, the complexities involved make such components unsuitable for the pilot project.

When the use of EDI is being planned, routine non-production items should not be ignored. Overalls, wipers, hand cleanser and grease are among items that can be ordered automatically. Long-term contracts are normally placed for such items with suppliers, and the storeman should be able to trigger a call-off order through a terminal. To prevent excessive stocks being built up—intentionally or not—orders can be matched against usage or stock levels. Just as EDI automates orders, eliminating unnecessary administration, so an integrated system allows stock to be controlled.

Any manufacturer will find that EDI is almost essential in controlling JIT deliveries from its suppliers, (See Chapter Four) and if the main reason for using EDI is to implement JIT, then a detailed strategy needs to be adopted. To start with, an audit of real stock levels—not those on the books—needs to be undertaken. Almost invariably, the true level of work-in-progress will be greater than expected. Apart from unexpected surplus stocks in the stores there is usually a number of obsolete parts gathering dust as well. Workers on assembly lines tend to keep a few extra sets of components under benches and in tool kits to prevent shortages from stopping the line as well. For the maximum benefit to be obtained, the stock level shown in the records need to be updated to take these extra components into account before JIT is implemented.

Starting the JIT/EDI programme

In deciding which components should be handled first in a JIT/EDI programme, value and bulk are clearly the criteria—bulk equals cost owing to the space dedicated to its storage. Unfortunately, most Western manufacturers lose some of the benefits of JIT because they do not use it between sections in their own plants. Although they may have reduced stock in the goods receiving warehouse by 75%, often the number of machined components or partly-assembled housings awaiting final assembly is unchanged. Without reducing work-in-progress of in-house materials and assemblies as much as stock in good receiving, manufacturers remain uncompetitive with their Japanese counterparts.

Recognising the weakness of this approach, Mitel Manufacturing Technologies (See Chapter Five) established a pull-type *Kanban* system to cut the levels of work-in-progress, at the same time as it started to use EDI to promote JIT for its bought-in components. This is the recommended approach for any manufacturer.

For any project to catch the confidence and enthusiasm of employees it must achieve success quickly, and EDI is no exception. The pilot programme must be a success, and the success should be broadcast to the employees so that they will expect it to be followed by a wider programme.

However, since EDI is a strategic move, it should not be introduced alone, but together with one or two other strategies aimed at improving efficiency. Rarely is a company in the situation where its management cannot see ways of improving the way it operates in a number of areas. By adopting several strategies, management will prepare the staff for change. It will be seen that the dedication is to improved performance, and not technology for its own sake. Typical of the strategies that might be adopted are:

- ☐ Simultaneous engineering, which leads to shorter time-to-market, better quality and lower costs;
- ☐ Total quality control, which requires a complete evaluation of the business, with all employees being involved;
- ☐ Zero defect programme;
- ☐ JIT or *Kanban* inside the factory;
- ☐ Bar coding of pallets;
- ☐ A change to cell manufacture and an elimination of unnecessary movement and space between successive processes;
- ☐ Changes in shift working or working practices.

The combination of a number of changes is just as relevant to a small manufacturer as it is to a large one. It may seem that EDI is enough innovation for the company to handle at one time, but since the other changes are concerned with methodology rather than technology, two or three projects can be handled together. All should be part of a strategy to raise operating efficiency.

It is important that EDI should be accepted quickly as an efficient new way of doing business that generates more changes than are apparent at first sight. The most important factors in starting EDI are:

- ☐ The technology should not be seen in isolation, but as a means of improving the way the business operates;
- ☐ Its use should be preceded by reviews of the company itself, its operations and paperwork;
- ☐ The pilot run should coincide with some other initiatives inside the company;
- ☐ The pilot programme must be shown to be successful, and its success broadcast internally;
- ☐ People should be trained in the acceptance and use of EDI.

With this approach, EDI will be accepted as the enabling technology it is, with its full use leading to strategic changes. However, there is one caveat: it is frequently said that 'EDI liberates people' as the paperwork is removed. That is true, but many people find those old routines and the heap of paper a comfortable way to work. Others prefer to be out chasing late deliveries than to be sitting at a desk watching a computer. Therefore, education is vitally important, while the working methods must be changed, but at a speed that the people involved can accept.

Chapter Fourteen

Expanding EDI into the future

High-speed data transmissions

CADCAM data by EDI

Satellite EDI for some transmissions

Few manual orders and payments by cheque

DEVELOPMENTS in EDI itself and in the liberalised telecommunications industry will expand use in the future. There are two main areas where change will come: in higher rates of data transmission, and in interactive EDI.

Within a few years, the ISDN network will be in general use by business, so that it will be commonplace for data to be transmitted at 64 kbit/s—25 times faster than is normal at present over a standard telephone line. Large manufacturers will be able to use multiples of the basic 64 kbit/s lines to transmit data much more quickly.
The reason that this multiplicity of rates will be practical is that ISDN is based on virtual lines passing down the same optical fibre cables between exchanges. Therefore, providing the lines between the subscriber and exchanges are also optical fibres, ultra-high speed data transmission will be practical.

Smart cards give security

In addition, smart cards, in which either a microprocessor and memory, or memory and a simple controller are embedded, allow great security for users. For example, the person that authorises electronic payments will be identified by the smart card, and the user may be asked not just for a password but also for some other identifying information hidden in the card before being allowed to sign on. The type of transaction that the user may make can also be embedded into the card. For example, an official may be able to authorise payments of certain amounts to given accounts only, and another may be able to authorise orders to a particular value. The cards can be tailored to suit the level of security a company considers necessary.

It is also expected that in a few years satellite EDI systems will be generally available for data transfers in Europe. With satellite systems, users will obtain a back-up system for the terrestrial lines, and will have the optimum system for sending data from one point to many points—satellites tend to be rather expensive for the transfer of data from point to point. Therefore, satellites are likely to be used for the distribution of:

☐ Workshop manuals and updated pages;
☐ Changes in prices for retailers;
☐ Changes in specification for retailers;
☐ Changes to replacement parts lists or prices;
☐ Information on recalls of faulty components;
☐ New product information.

In all these cases, the existing situation is unsatisfactory because companies cannot be sure that all dealers will implement the data they receive at the same time. Therefore, a considerable lag is allowed from the time the data is despatched to the implementation date. This can be overcome to some extent by the use of courier services, but where data has to be entered into a computer or manual, more time can be lost.

With EDI, the changes will be made automatically on receipt, with the new file relegating the old one to back-up status.

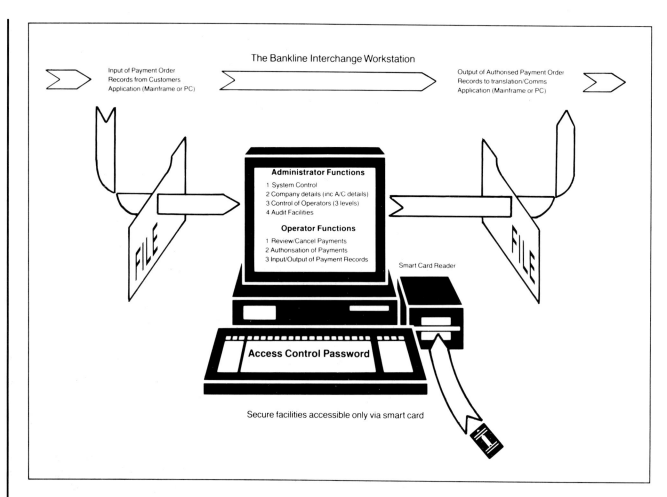

The Bankline Interchange Workstation

Input of Payment Order
Records from Customers
Application (Mainframe or PC)

Output of Authorised Payment Order
Records to translation/Comms
Application (Mainframe or PC)

Administrator Functions

1 System Control
2 Company details (inc A/C details)
3 Control of Operators (3 levels)
4 Audit Facilities

Operator Functions

1 Review/Cancel Payments
2 Authorisation of Payments
3 Input/Output of Payment Records

Smart Card Reader

Access Control Password

Secure facilities accessible only via smart card

Fig. 14.1. A password, smart card and card reader are needed to authorise electronic fund transfers. This is the approach proposed by National Westminster Bank

It is likely that some industries will emulate the aim of the CALS project (See Chapter Two) and keep their workshop manuals on disc, with the sections being downloaded to a service shop when needed. In this way, the danger of obsolete manuals being used will be eliminated.

The general use by business of smart cards will make the widespread use of EFT (electronic fund transfers) from manufacturers to vendors and from dealers to manufacturers practical. Cheques will disappear from the business scene, and some companies will set up small groups to handle financial settlements by EDI, using banks less than at present.

The use of self-billing and EFT for payments will have a significant effect on the manning levels in administrative departments, and will improve relations between manufacturers and vendors. The remark 'the cheque is in the post' will disappear from business.

EFT completes cycle

As with any other areas that EDI touches, a business cycle including EFT reduces the number of transactions involved, and the likelihood for errors. Normally, a vendor sends an invoice to the customer's accounts department soon after it has sent the advice note with the delivery to the goods receiving department. Accounts, which is receiving hundreds of invoices each day, needs to match up the invoice with the advice note, making sure that there are discrepancies in neither the agreed price nor in the quantity. If all is well, it sends a

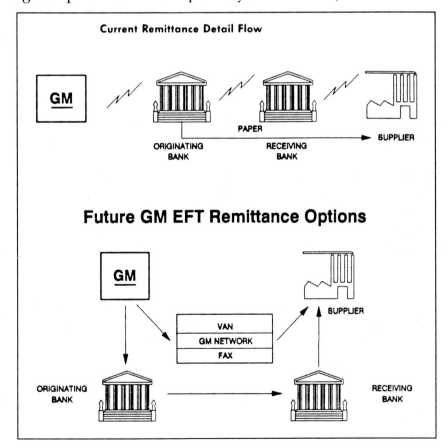

Fig. 14.2. Because few banks were using EDI when GM started to make payments by EFT, some processes involved paper. In the future, EDI users will make most payments electronically

remittance advice to the vendor, and some time later sends a cheque. However, if there was a discrepancy between the invoice and advice note, adjustments are made, and the cheque may take a long time to materialise. When the vendor receives the remittance advice it may consider it to be incorrect, so a new period of negotiations begin—and these are all supposedly routine transactions.

With EDI, the vendor sends the advance shipping notice, the bar code is read at goods receiving, and errors at this stage are few. Data from the bar code label is transferred directly—not keyed in—to accounts which uses that data as a basis for raising a self-billing invoice, combined with remittance advice which is sent to the vendor. Later, it authorises the bank to make a payment by EFT.

Of course, there is still room for errors, but now those relating to price are handled directly by the purchasing department, and those relating to quantity by production control. Accounts is not involved directly.

There is still room for a remittance advice to be queried by the vendor. However, since the same data are used throughout, and the data from the bar code label are matched automatically to the advance shipping note, the whole procedure is not only more accurate but much simpler.

And, the number of transactions is reduced. At least five transactions by mail are replaced by three by EDI. Since the five transactions are sequential, six-eight weeks is the minimum practical delay from the submission of the invoice to the cheque being received by the vendor. With EDI, that period can be cut to five-eight days, and four of those days can be included to allow the vendor to query the remittance advice note/self-billing invoice. In practice, payments are not likely to be made that quickly, but they will be made regularly, perhaps three weeks after delivery, instead of 12-15 weeks after.

Interactive EDI

In EDI technology itself, one extra service that is required in some situations is one in which the user can ask questions. Currently, orthodox EDI is batch processed—that is, the data are sent to a bureau where they are processed in a batch with other data. Then, the partner receives the data. However, there is another form of EDI called interactive EDI or IEDI, in which a user can interrogate its partner's computer. Types of interactive EDI are already in use in the airline and other industries for bookings. IEDI does not replace EDI, but it will take over certain aspects of the business. For example, IEDI is needed for communications with the Customs authorities, owing to the complex rules and tariffs now in use. With IEDI, Customs can vet a declaration, and either approve it or send back queries. Without IEDI, the system could take too long, negating some of the other benefits. The same approach could be used when a manufacturer wishes to know whether a vendor has a component in stock, or can supply a non-standard or non-production item.

IEDI will also allow dealers to interrogate stock levels at the factory and at other dealers, and to gain answers to technical queries from customers or service departments. Companies should also be able to interrogate their trading partner's computer to obtain answers to queries relating to deliveries or discrepancies in quantities.

IEDI differs from EDI in that the amounts of data involved are small because a question is usually sent; the response triggers another question and so on. Therefore, standards for IEDI will differ from those for EDI. Their development will open up new business opportunities.

CADCAM data by EDI

For manufacturers, the development of ISDN to allow CAD or CAM data to be transmitted economically, and forge even closer links between members of the supply chain. Early in the simultaneous engineering programme, the manufacturer will be able to send outline details of a design to key vendors—at this stage possibly by satellite—and owing to the speed of transmission, will be able to transmit updates regularly. This facility will not replace the meetings that are essential with simultaneous engineering, but will supplement them, allowing vendors to arrive with their latest drawings, which they have transmitted to the customer just before the meeting, so that all members of the simultaneous engineering team will be able to discuss them.

Manufacturers will need to clarify the ownership of such data, and how the vendor is permitted to use them beforehand. Obviously, if a company is to transmit data concerning a product due to be marketed in three years' time, it will need to be certain the vendor will respect its confidence—once again, for the system to function effectively, trust is needed.

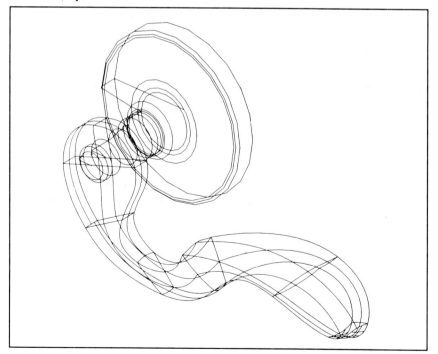

Fig. 14.3. Not only will CAD data be transmitted by EDI in the future, but EDI will allow designers at different sites to work together simultaneously on the same drawing

Interactive design sessions

In addition, when a critical stage in a design is reached, the design draughtsmen at the manufacturer and vendor will be able to sit at workstations in different towns, and see the same component on screen. They will be able to call up an interactive mode, in which case as one adds a line to the screen, the other will see it instantaneously on his screen. Thus, the two designers will be able to work together, improving the design more quickly than is possible at present.

Simultaneous engineering is the key to shortening time-to-market, and will become a more effective tool with interactive EDI for CAD. Not only will designs be produced more quickly, but relations between vendor and customer will improve.

In manufacture, the use of bar codes will be integrated with EDI to automate ordering. As the pallet at the side of the line is emptied, the operator will press a couple of keys on the scanner, and scan the bar code so that the data are sent back to the warehouse. Then, a new pallet will be sent, and the empty one returned to the warehouse—on an automated guided vehicle—while the data are transmitted back to the computer in administration.

The stock level will be compared automatically with the production schedule, and if the component is one in continuous use, a new order will be placed on the vendor. If a different component is required for the next batch, it will be ordered automatically; but if there is some doubt, the purchasing officer's attention will be drawn to the computer screen, so that he or she can decide what to do.

Orders automated

The key to the future in this area will be the absence of orders; retailers will use data from EPOS terminals to order replacements automatically, and manufacturers will use similar systems. People will need to deal only with shortages or special situations.

To cope with the changing situation, vendors and stockholders will maintain databases of stock levels, and lead times for components. These databases will allow customers to compare one with another, leading to those offering shorter lead times to gain increased market share. At the same time, stockholders will be able to make special offers to clear old stock. These developments lead to automated ordering.

Databases for industry

Some providers of information will offer industry-wide databases through interactive EDI, so that subscribers will be able to compare different products and services and choose accordingly. Vendors' performance will be transparent—the veils resulting from a lack of information will be torn away, revealing just which vendors are efficient and which are not.

With the combination of automated EDI and automated factories, the supply chain becomes close to the ideal of a continuous production line. The virtual factory will actually extend beyond the chain of vendors involved continuously in the production schedules of a manufacturer, to those required for occasional products only. In all cases, the factories and the hauliers used between them will provide integrated manufacture, offering very short lead times and high quality in a great variety of products. For any manufacturing company, then, the use of EDI is the essential prelude to a future bristling with opportunities. □

EDI glossary

AECMA Aerospace Europe EDI group

ANSI American National Standards Institute. The ANSI X.12 standard defines message structures, syntax and data elements for EDI, and is used principally in North America

ANA Article Number Association, the UK Association that publishes and maintains the UK EAN coding systems and Tradacoms EDI standards

Bit/s Rate of transfer of data in bits/second; each character consists of eight bits. Modems can transfer data at rates from 300 to 2,400 bit/s normally, and at 9,600 bit/s in some cases. ISDN allows transfer at 64kbit/s (64,000 bit/s)

BSI British Standards Institution

BSI IST/14 British Standards Institution Information and Systems Technology, a committee dealing with data elements and syntaxes for EDI. The Secretariat is provided by SITPRO

CCITT Committee Consultative International Telegraphique et Telephonique, the body of PTTs that sets international standards for telephony

Cefic Confederation of European Chemical Industries, a European EDI system initiated in 1987 by 12 major chemical manufacturers committed to Edifact and X.400 Data element Data elements are combined to form messages

Cost 306 EEC EDI initiative for transport

Deupro Ausschuss fur die Vereinfachung internationaler Handelsverfahren in der Europaischen Gemeinschaft, the German committee for the simplification of trade procedures

EAN International numbering and barcoding association

EAN-COM EDI messages developed by EAN for its members

EDI Electronic Data Interchange

EDIA Electronic Data Interchange Association

Edicon A British EDI community for the construction industry committed to Edifact

Edifact EDI for Administration Commerce and Trade. Edifact consists of a set of international standards developed by a United Nations working party that brought together UN-GTDI and ANSI X.12

Edifice EDI forum for companies with Interests in Computing and Electronics which supports Edifact

Edis EDI association for transport and harbours

Ediship EDI initiative between export/import companies and shipping lines for booking invoicing and transmission of bills of lading

EFT Electronic funds transfer, usually by banks

EFTPOS Electronic funds transfer at the point of sale

Electronic Trading EDI + electronic mail + other interactive functions

Emedi European medical EDI linking the British NHS with French and Dutch partners

EPOS Electronic point of sale (terminal)

ISDN Integrated Service Digital Network, the telecommunications system allowing transmission of voice, data, fax and video images over the same digital lines

ISO 7372 The International Standard Organisation's trade data element directory, identical to the UN version

ISO 9735 The International Standard Organisation's syntax standard, identical to Edifact syntax

Limnet Lloyds network for insurance EDI

Message An identified structured set of data elements and segments covering the requirements for a specified transaction

Odette The Organisation for Data Exchange for Teletransmission in Europe. An organisation for developing EDI standards principally for the motor industry in eight European countries, now moving toward the use of Edifact

OSI Open Systems Interconnection, a set of principles agreed internationally to allow computers of different makes to communicate

PC Personal computer

PDN Public data network. Protocol Rules and conventions under which systems operate - generally for transmission by telecommunications

PSS Packet switched service

Rinet The international reinsurance network set up in 1987 by leading reinsurance companies

Simpofrance Comite Francaise pour la simplification des procedures du commerce international, the French committee for the simplification of trade procedures

SITPRO Simpler Trade Procedures Board, supported by the UK Department of Trade and Industry

SNA Systems network architecture, a data communications protocol developed by IBM

TEDIS Trade electronic data interchange systems, an EC programme for EDI implementation

Tradacoms Business message standards for EDI developed by ANA and conforming to UN-TDI

Unece United Nations Economic Commission for Europe, involved in the development of EDI

UN/ECE/WP.4 United Nations Economic Commission for Europe Working Party No 4 on Facilitation of International Trade Procedures which is responsible for the development of international EDI standards, UN/Edifact

UN-TDI UN standards for Trade Data Interchange

UNGTDI-UN Guidelines for Trade Data Interchange and the original European standards for data interchange

UNSM United Nations Standards Message; messages approved by the UN Edifact working party

UNTDED United Nations trade data element directory, part of which constitutes ISO 7372. It includes the standard data elements and associated codes and is maintained jointly by the UN Secretariat and ISO

UNTDID United Nations trade data interchange directory

VADS Value added data service

VAN Value added network, which is not only a network for transmission of data but also storage and manipulation of data to suit different trading partners

X.12 Standard for EDI adopted by ANSI

X.25 Protocol for transmission over PDN

X.400 Protocol for data transmission for messages of any type, and to be output in any form, including facsimile and telex

Further reading

EDI Technology, edited by M Gifkins, published by Blenheim Online Publications

Electronic Data Interchange: Managing implementation in a purchasing environment, by R M Monczka and J R Carter, National Association of Purchasing Management, USA

The organizational aspects of EDI: a project manager's guide by N F Barber, published by TDCC: The Electronic Data Interchange Association

The EDIFACT Service, published by SITPRO, Venture House, 29 Glasshouse St, London W1R 5RG

Simultaneous Engineering: the management guide (1st Edition 1990, 2nd Edition 1991) by John Hartley, published by Industrial Newsletters Ltd, 42 Market Square, Toddington Beds, UK

EDI'90 proceedings of the conference held 30 October-1 November at the Queen Elizabeth II Conference Centre, London

EDI and X.400 using Pedi, an implementors and users guide by Richard Hill, published by Technology Appraisal Ltd, 551 London Rd, Isleworth, Middx TW7 4DS, UK

The EDI Project planner, published by EDI Executive Publications, 1639 Desford Court, Marietta, GA 30064, USA

EDI in Europe: the Business Opportunity published by Ovum Ltd, 7 Rathbone St London W1P1AF, UK

TEDIS, Trade Electronic Data Interchange Systems - a Community programme for co-operation, available from the Commission of the European Communities in English, German, Spanish, Italian and French

EDI in perspective (EUR 11883, 1989), published by the EEC

Factsheets on EDI (EUR 12293, 1989), published by the EEC

Report on the EDI legal workshop, Brussels, 19-20 June 1989, published by the EEC

Report on EDI security workshop, Brussels 20-21 June 1989, published by the EEC

Report on EDI telecommunications workshop, Brussels 22-23 June 1989, published by the EEC

Proceedings of the TEDIS conference, Brussels 12-13 July 1989

Legal Situation in the Member States regarding trade electronic data interchange, September 1989, XIII/D/6/7-90, published by the EEC

Survey of EDI in all the Member States 1989, XIII/D/5/6-90, published by the EEC

Acknowledgements

The author would like to express his thanks to the following companies and organisations for their help in the preparation of this book:
AT&T Istel, Black & Decker, B&Q, British Coal, Coats Viyella, Digital Equipment, Ford Motor Co, IBM, INS, Lucas Automotive, Mitel Manufacturing Technologies, Tesco, Rover Group, Rowntree Mackintosh, and SMMT.

He would also like to thank the following for illustrations:
AT&T Istel, BPCC Numeric Arts, Computervision, Digital Equipment Corporation, Ford Motor Co, IBM, National Westminster Bank plc, SD-Scicon, SMMT, TEDIS for two Figs. from 'EDI in Perspective', Vistec Business Systems and EDI Group Ltd, for permisson to use Figs. 12.3 and 14.2 from 'EDI FORUM' journal.

Notes

Index